DAVE BECK

John D. McCallum

The Writing Works, Inc.
Mercer Island, Washington

Gordon Soules Book Publishers
Vancouver, B.C., Canada

Library of Congress Cataloging in Publication Data

McCallum, John Dennis, 1924-
  Dave Beck.

  Includes index.
  1. Beck, Dave, 1894—   2. Trade-unions—United
States—Officials and employees—Biography.   3. International Brotherhood of Teamsters, Chauffeurs, Warehousemen and Helpers of America.
HD6509.B42A35   1978   331.88'11'3883240924   [B]
ISBN 0-916076-27-X   78-11819

Manufactured in the United States
Published by The Writing Works, Inc.
            7438 S.E. 40th Street
            Mercer Island, Washington 98040
ISBN: 0-916076-27-X (United States)
Library of Congress Catalog Card Number: 78-11819

Published in Canada by Gordon Soules Book Publishers
   1118-355 Burrard Street
     Vancouver, B.C., Canada V6C 2G8
ISBN: 0-919574-23-8 (Canada)

Contents

ACKNOWLEDGMENTS

I wish to thank Ann Watkins Kotin, who was Dave Beck's private secretary for 31 years and so graciously shared her private memories of him; and to William M. Griffin, Susan Gerrard, Edith Strash, and Audrey E. Neil for their assistance in the editing of the manuscript.

TO
DOROTHY, HELEN,
AND DAVE JR.

*Judge Tom Mercer, who arrived in Seattle in 1852, brought with him the town's first team of horses and became the first teamster. Years later, Nard Jones, the author and newspaperman, asked Dave Beck if he knew the name of Seattle's first teamster, and when he hesitated, Nard told him the story of Judge Mercer. "By god," cried Beck, roaring with laughter, "and all this time I thought it was **me**!"*

1
Beck
Is Back

DAVE BECK, whose evangelical zeal was his trademark back in the 1950s as one of the most powerful labor leaders in America, has been relatively quiet in recent years; so quiet, as a matter of fact, that a good many people thought he was dead.

But the old Teamster boss is very much alive. Now at 84, he has slipped off the 16-ounce gloves for bare knuckles and is ready to clear the air. It's good to have him back. He wants to get some old business off his chest—feelings he has had cooped up inside him since he got out of federal prison in 1964.

At one stage of our many conversations, he said, "Am I being too rough?"

"Not at all," I told him. "That's a different breed out there. They don't shock easily."

"Well," he said, "I want to be fair. I don't want it to sound like some old guy gone sour on the world."

"You want to shake up a few people, don't you?"

"Yes," he said. "But I don't want to be too sensational. I can stir them up without resorting to that stuff."

"Just speak your mind," I told him. "Just call the shots the way you see them."

"Well," he said, "when I'm through here, I want them to be able to sit back and say, 'By golly, he's right.'"

"Right or wrong," I said, "it's time you talked. It's time you tell your side of the story."

"No Fifth Amendments?"

"No, sir."

"Well," he said, "let's go to work."

And the critics, be damned.

When listening to Beck, his words are not fancy; neither are they obscure. You never have to try to figure out what he is up to; he tells you what he is up to. He is as direct and forceful as a left jab to the mouth. At 84 he still criticizes his detractors to their faces and has outspoken contempt for most modern politicians, but he mixes his criticisms and opinions with old-fashioned spunk and wit that at once wins him the attention of his audience. Reporters learned long ago that when angry or provoked, Dave will talk for hours at a stretch with much resultant hot copy. His reactions have not changed much down the years. When I first met with him to arrange a work schedule for this book, his rapid-fire, nonstop oratory was six jumps ahead of my pencil. To add to the confusion, he was very animated, illustrating each point with a phantom jab and gesticulation. So at sessions that followed, a tape cassette captured his fiery speech verbatim, leaving me free to duck the accentuating rights and lefts and to shoot my own questions across. That recorder holds history's first oratorical decision over Beck. He quit after five hours of steady talking.

During our taping sessions, incidentally, there were few subjects on which he said, "I'd rather not get into that," or, "Let's leave that out." He never stopped to calculate his words so as to put the best possible construction on potentially negative matters. On all phases of his highly controversial life, the details flowed out with the characteristic spontaneity of this man who doesn't try to fool anybody, including himself. "Leave the chips fall where they may," became his credo. "At my age, what have I got to lose?"

Beck's memory is his greatest single asset. He remembers almost everything he ever learned, including the unpleasant things. And as he recreated his life for me—reminiscing out loud for hours at a time, day after day, the high points of his life as well as the low periods—my cassette was there to capture precisely all his words and opinions and attitudes. Nothing was left to the fallible memory and notebook of the collaborator.

The Dave Beck of 1978 has not changed much from the Dave Beck who joined the Teamsters more than six decades ago. He still arises at 6 a.m. and still puts in a 12-hour day managing his real estate holdings. After a recent physical, his doctor pronounced him "abnormally healthy—get out of here."

It has been written that every man's life ends the same way, and it is only the details of how he lived and how he died that distinguishes any of us. Briefly, Dave Beck became general president of the Teamsters Union in 1952 and led it during its fastest growth period. In 1962 he was sent to federal prison. He served 30 months at McNeil Island, then in 1964 was paroled. In 1975 President Gerald Ford granted him a full pardon. Beck has continued to insist upon his innocence, saying he never saw a report that served as the basis for the conviction, but because he was president he was technically responsible. A lot of Beck sympathizers felt that the two and a half years he spent in prison was a hell of a bum rap to pin on him. Others felt it wasn't long enough. Pro, anti, or neutral, a large corps of the curious, including a battalion of TV and newspaper reporters and news photographers, were on the dock to meet the prison boat that brought Beck back to the mainland.

Beck knew a lot of the press corps by their first names. Yes, he told them, he was glad to be free. No, he said, he didn't hold any grudges against those who put him behind prison walls. His weight? About 40 pounds lighter than when he went in.

"And what are your immediate plans?" somebody wanted to know.

"I'll settle in Seattle," Dave said. "I've had a couple of business offers, nothing definite yet. And then there's a book. Publishers are after me to get a collaborator and write a book about my life. There are a lot of things I want to get off my chest."

So now—14 years later—here, finally, is that book.

2

Dave Beck: One Man's Opinion

DAVE BECK sat in his favorite stuffed chair in a corner of his living room and talked in a steady, staccato stream of words—a curious, animated monologue that touched on a variety of subjects, amplifying, adding color and detail. His skin was lobster-pink and healthy-looking, and his blue eyes were amused and bright. Except for a slight paunch, he looked 20 years younger than his 84 years. His arms were still thick and muscular. He kept himself in shape, he told me, by jogging several times a week. He neither smoked nor drank—never did. The years had been good to him. He looked just as feisty and mischievous and forthright as he had when he was running the Teamsters in the mid-1950s and was generally regarded as one of the most powerful union leaders in America.

He looked like a man who enjoyed himself hugely and who, if he did not, kept that knowledge to himself. Nothing embarrassed him. McNeil Island? Sure, he spent time at the federal pen—30 months, in fact. Best vacation he ever had, he said. Jimmy Hoffa? No, he didn't know where his former aide might be, but wherever he was, he wasn't talking. The Teamsters today? He had no comment since he takes no part in their administrative affairs.

Years ago, when Beck was the Teamsters' No. 1 organizer, he surrounded himself with rough, tough people who could take care of themselves in a street fight. Joe Gottstein, the horse track executive, came to Dave one day and told about some problems a nephew of his was having back in Minneapolis.

Joe said, "The Dunn brothers are in there from Butte, Montana, and are pushing your truck drivers all over the place. Dave, you should do something."

Dave was on his way to a board meeting in Washington, D.C.

"Don't worry," he told Gottstein. "I'll talk to Dan Tobin at the board meeting." Tobin was president of the Teamsters.

Later, Beck asked Tobin how long was he going to stand by and allow the Dunns to push the Teamsters around. One word led to another and, finally, Tobin exploded. "Dammit, Dave," he said, "I suppose you think you could settle the issue."

Dave said, "I know positively I can settle it, but only with the understanding that I will have sole authority with no interference from anyone. I will bring in 40 or 50 of my own trained personnel from the West Coast and they will handle everything associated with this cleanup of Minneapolis. We have built the Western Conference of Teamsters with a structure that adheres to the principles of sound business dealing, with capital investment, the welfare of the consumer, and adherence to the principles of the trade union movement. We will not tolerate actions such as the Dunns have carried on in Minneapolis. Such actions are destructive to everyone—business, capital investment, the workers. If the Dunns want to write a rule book along the lines they have been following, then we will play within that rule book, but it's their choice, not ours."

The rest is history. The Dunns were compelled to leave Minneapolis. With the full support of Central Conference officials, the job was accomplished so successfully that Dave was invited to make the principal address at the installation of the newly elected Chamber of Commerce president.

"Business, labor, and industry had successfully accomplished this action," Beck recalls. "Our progress in Minneapolis from that day forward has always been continuous and progressive, measured in wages, hours and conditions."

In the months after our first meeting, Dave Beck and I had days, sometimes weeks, of conversations, most of them on tape, some not.

"Dad blast it," he'd roar, his round, florid face twisted with anger. "An outrage," and he'd be off and lashing out at such old adversaries as the late Bobby Kennedy, and Harry Bridges. Other times his voice remained quiet, gentle, tea-time social, as he talked thoughtfully about the future of the Teamsters. "Our ideal president must have tremendous administrative ability and *militancy*," he'd say. "He should also come up from the ranks of the truck drivers. I once drove a laundry truck in the early days of the union—when guys like Estes were building the Teamsters—when the union was so raw it couldn't even get bank credit. Why, for the first 50 years of its existence, the trucking industry never got any financial help from the banks. It wasn't a business even recognized by banks. Therefore, I'd want a man who came up the hard way, is familiar with the union's embattled history, and actually has had experience on a truck. I don't believe you can have the true feel or spirit of the labor movement based on a purely academic background."

Tobin, Beck, Hoffa, and Fitzsimmons all came up through the ranks of the Teamsters.

In an attempt to put his story into perspective, Beck suggested I talk to others—people who have followed his

career—intimates who have known him best. One of those
I talked to was Don Duncan, for 14 years a featured col-
umnist for the *Seattle Times* and now managing editor of
the *Tacoma News Tribune*. Duncan has been a Beck
observer most of his life. Like any Seattle boy who grew up
during the depression, he had heard the name of Dave
Beck spoken around the dinner table from the time he was
old enough to stop taking naps.

"Dave had the working man at heart," Duncan said.
"Tough, fist-pounding, garrulous, street-wise, there were
stories about him using muscle to organize the Teamsters.
There were stories, too, about some of his associates. His
assistants were held in awe.

"But," Don Duncan continued, "it wasn't until Bobby
Kennedy zeroed in on Beck in those old Senate subcommittee investigations on racketeering of the mid-1950s that
I saw Dave—in the flesh—sweating under the lights and
taking the Fifth Amendment. The man who had been
honored by Seattle businessmen and then, in essence, fed
to the hounds with a smile was not a very pretty sight on
national TV. I found myself feeling sorry for Dave. Crazy.
But that's the way it was.

"I remember a great picture that came out of those
days. Dave had returned to Seattle after the hearings, and
the press was waiting at the airport for him. Dave's son, a
big hulk of a man, was there, and he grabbed his father's
hand as if to take him away from it all. The late Hack
Miller of the *Seattle P-I* caught it all on film, and the
late Sam Angeloff wrote the perfect caption: 'Father, dear
Father, come home with me now.' It won the top Sigma
Delta Chi Excellence in Journalism Award in Washington
State that year."

Duncan's first face-to-face meeting with Dave oc-
curred after he had gotten out of the federal penitentiary at
McNeil Island near Tacoma. Everybody wanted to see
Beck, to interview him. Dave Beck was big news.

"Heck," Duncan said, "you couldn't get a telephone

number, and he never has had his name listed on the roster of tenants in the apartment building where he lives —'right above where I used to deliver newspapers on the street corner,' he likes to say. Anyway, I got hold of an attorney who said he'd tell Dave I wanted to see him. I was writing a daily column for the *Seattle Times* by then. One day the phone rang and I heard, 'Hello, Don; this is Dave Beck. Sure, I'll see you. Name the time.' Off I went, accompanied by my photographer George Carkonen. Dave was much shorter than I had expected. Roly poly. A face with those unlined, pudgy cheeks like Winston Churchill, who once said, 'All rosy babies look like me.' I got some nifty quotes from Dave. There was a really good one: 'I could drive from Seattle to Tacoma and throw my hat out of the window on Highway 99, near Federal Way. Wherever that hat landed I could buy the property and make a fine profit.' Subsequent events proved he was right as rain. Whatever his success is in business today, can be attributed to his investments in real estate.

"Then, the *coup de grace*. Dave was talking about his exercise bicycle—to keep trim—and I said, 'Hey, get on it and let George take some pictures.' He has always kept himself in top physical shape—the one thing he gained from McNeil Island, he said, was the opportunity to continue to exercise regularly. He agreed to pose, then stripped to the waist, and pumped away, talking all the time. George fired flashbulbs a mile a minute. I figured any second Dave will realize that he's going to be on every front page in the country.

"We finally left. The pictures were great. *Time* magazine used one of them. The story was pretty good, too.

We didn't see each other again for quite awhile. I covered Dave once when he spoke to a class, political science, I believe, at the University of Washington. This was 'living history' and the students ate it up.

"Now and then Dave dropped me a note when I moved over to the *Tacoma News Tribune*. As managing editor, I assigned somebody to cover him when he spoke to a Grange group in Pierce County. Then when Dave finally got that Presidential pardon, I wrote the front page story after getting some good quotes by phone from Dave. I was very happy for him, because it seemed to be the dream that had been sustaining him. After that I guess I figured he'd just fade away. But he keeps going on. Quite recently, I contacted him about a story I was doing on Senator Henry M. Jackson. Dave invited me back to his apartment. Things were piled around. But Dave looked pretty much the same. He has always had a remarkable memory, and he can talk for hours nonstop. We talked about Jackson; Dave said the senator was sincere, dedicated, and that he had contributed to his campaigns. He also spoke warmly about Senator Warren Magnuson, a former member of his union who worked his way through Law School at the University of Washington delivering ice. There were other things—mostly private things—about people in Seattle who used power and the deals they made. Dave came down pretty hard on Sea-First Bank, which, he said, he had helped by pulling Teamster money out of Indianapolis banks and giving it to Seattle back when he was a power. But Sea-First forgot that when Beck really needed help. Fortunately, his friends did not. He also talked about buying land in Washington, D.C., for the International Teamsters headquarters—worth millions now. And he said that quote about throwing his hat out the window—from our long-ago interview—was remembered by people every day. He said he finally had worked out his problems with the IRS—all caused by the death of his first wife.

"We said goodbye. I was again surprised at how short he was—I always imagined him to be 10-feet tall—and at the softness of his hand. It is a shame that people like Dave Beck and our colorful former Lieutenant Governor and Secretary of State Victor Aloysius Meyers couldn't go around to the schools and talk to the kids and let them know how it was back then when the newsmakers were always a little bigger than life."

Dave Beck never really got out of the streets where he grew up—where he sold newspapers. He lives very close to the late Joshua Green's famous mansion. He often walks downtown to the banks and walks back up the hill again, waving to his friends as he comes and goes. From where he sits on the 12th floor of his apartment house on top of a hill, he can look out the big windows and see the tall buildings and all the changes that have been wrought in his town, especially since the 1962 World's Fair. He can look out over that beautiful Seattle harbor and see the ferries and the big ships and the tugboats come and go like shimmering diamonds on the water. Seattle, where Dave is, *smells* of salt water. When you come over the mountains from eastern Washington—when you get to the top of the pass—you say to yourself, "Hey, you can smell the salt water." You're about 50 or 60 miles from salt water, but you can still smell it. Dave Beck can smell it, too—and he *feels* it.

Seattle, of course, has always been a great labor town. It was the home of the first—and only—general strike in any major city in the history of the United States, back in the days of Anna Louise Strong.

"Funny thing about Dave," Don Duncan said, "when talking to him, you get this feeling he's a conservative. Sitting on his living room coffee table are all these magazines: *Business Week, Time, Newsweek, U.S. News & World Report, Forbes, Wall Street Journal.* But Dave has always maintained that capital and labor must work together with the human equation of labor as their contribution, the other as financial to build a strong and powerful America. He believed in getting money for the working man, granted, but he also believed in seeing a company survive. He didn't want to kill the goose that laid the golden egg. This, I believe, has been a part of Beck. He certainly hasn't been anti-business. In his prime, he looked like a man who wanted to see the American economy grow—and the working man with it.

"If anyone ever does a history of the Pacific Northwest, the name Dave Beck has to rank higher than the bankers—higher than the politicians—higher than almost anyone. We are probably the best organized area in America, thanks to Beck. Someone once referred to America as 'the 47 states and the Soviet of Washington.' Of course, we've always been the great labor capital of the country. My own great grandfather was a member of the Wobblies—worked in the logging camps. I once asked him what being a Wobbly meant. He said, 'No bed bugs in your blankets and maybe some breakfast cereal that isn't tainted.' That's all the workingman wanted back in those days—a warm bed and a square meal.

"'That's all business gave them in those days,' Beck said. 'They also kept the black man in slavery until it created civil revolution in our country and cost the lives of hundreds of thousands of our citizens.'

"Dave's an amazing guy. You can ask him a question and he'll say, 'I can't say a word about that,' and then he proceeds to totally unload on the subject. He can be very candid—and also very mum. There are certain areas that seem to be private to him. Jimmy Hoffa is one. On the subject of Hoffa, he's very guarded. Dave doesn't talk about women, either, except to put them on a pedestal. I don't think I ever heard anything more than a 'hell' or a 'damn' from Dave whenever a woman is around. I've never heard a dirty four-letter word come out of him; I've never heard him tell a smutty story. He's never smoked, never touched liquor. Those habits are not a part of Beck, the salacious stuff. Key-hole peeping is not Dave Beck. What he likes is power—he'd like to feel he's as powerful today as he ever was. But at 84, he's realistic. He knows better.

"As a newspaperman, I can tell you that Dave Beck has always been popular with the press. He's had his battles with reporters, sure, but there's nothing personal about it. He'll call you up, drop you a note, and sign it Dave. I've got all my Dave Beck notes saved, because those signatures are some day going to be as valuable as anything I've ever gotten from a President.

"To fully understand Dave Beck, you must understand the Seattle of the long-ago; the way it was when he was growing up. In those days people were identified by their neighborhoods. I was the kid from Beacon Hill, for example—Italians, Slavs, Poles, and for a while, Japanese. Every part of Seattle had its unique character. There was Broadmoor, where the wealthy lived. Magnolia Bluff and West Seattle were fine residential neighborhoods, with West Seattle in the early days relying on ferry service to reach the city. And Ballard, that's where all the Swedes lived—and the Norwegians. They all went fishing, and they went fishing every year. They did a bit of logging, too, but basically, Ballard was fish-eating territory.

"So there they were, every part of Seattle had its own area, its own peculiar personality. Dave Beck? Every man would like to have a city that's tailor-made for him. And I think Seattle was the perfect stage for Dave to act out his drama—to organize labor—to grow—to dream—to live. It was right for him and vice versa. Seattle was not too many years removed from the logs and tall trees growing right down to the waterfront—right down to the shores of Lake Washington. And a go-getter like Dave Beck was there, just getting started, ready to build a city.

"Dave Beck was the first nationally-recognized figure to come out of the Pacific Northwest. Homer T. Bone, who gave us public power, may have had more impact on the area, but he wasn't as well known throughout the country as Beck. Three times Beck met in private with Sir Winston Churchill—twice in London, once in Miami, Florida. Three times Presidents wanted to make him Secretary of Labor—Roosevelt, Truman, and Eisenhower.

"Dave was always a great actor. He reminds me of Clay Nixon, the attorney who always had a marvelous knack of playing to the audience. One day I saw Clay stand up in court and say to a jury, 'Don't let your prejudices send this little Armenian to prison,' while tears were pouring down his cheeks. I asked him afterwards how he did it. 'Well,' he said, 'a little garlic in the handkerchief doesn't hurt.'

"Summing up, there just aren't very many Dave Becks around. He's unique. He's special. From the fringes, Dave gives the impression of a power figure—unlovable—gruff—a lion. But when you get close to him, you say to yourself, 'My god, here's a Kewpie Doll.' I'm sure others feel it too. He's really a helluva guy. He just doesn't look like a heavy. And yet, he must have said things behind closed doors that made things happen. He must have been tougher than Billy Hell at times. That was a very tough league he played in. And yet, you never see that side of him when he's on stage. Hoffa? I don't think Jimmy ever saw the day when he was as big or as powerful as Dave Beck. There's just no comparison. Hoffa was a totally different type who came along at a different time. Hell, Dave Beck wasn't going to wind up in a hunk of concrete. Good gosh, at 84 he's still collecting a pension of $50,000 a year."

3

Beck Watchers

THE WORDS of Don Duncan were still fresh in my head when I was introduced to this priest, a Jesuit from Seattle. "Yes," he said, "I knew Dave Beck." He had been educated in the great universities of America and Europe with doctorates in economics and labor relations. "Beck has always fascinated me," he continued. "I knew him before he went to Washington, while he was there, and afterward." He was willing to talk for the record.

"Listen," the priest said, "I don't see any reason to be too hard on Beck. In your book, be sure to bring out how the government went after him. I'm sure it was the political procedures of Bobby Kennedy. Unions have gone downhill since Beck's time, partly because they are too lazy to organize. They sit back, waiting for the union shop to sign up people for them. Beck went after new members. During 1952-1957 when he headed the Teamsters, he organized more than a half-million workers. That's more than the Teamsters have organized in the 20 years since Beck retired."

The priest glanced at the ceiling, mouth pursed, thinking.

"Truck drivers earn every penny they get," he said. "They work long, arduous hours—not like some in the building trades. Beck knows. He once drove a laundry truck himself. He came up the hard way. Like George Meany, I always figured Beck had a limited education and believed the unions were all-powerful. When the McClellan committee started investigating unions, Beck was asked a question about his methods of running the Teamsters. As I remember, Dave felt so completely cocksure of himself, he replied, 'Senator Ives, you have a good prounion record. We aren't out to get you!' That was the height of rather innocent arrogance."

At the time of the Senate Rackets Committee, the priest said he was living in Portland, Oregon, and Bobby Kennedy came out from Washington, D.C., to personally look into coin machine operations in that state. "They got nowhere," the priest said. "So they tried to find some slim connection with Beck—real smear tactics. Charges would be made or associations hinted at by Bobby on TV. Bobby'd ruin a person's name, then move quickly on having proven nothing. I think Bobby's role should play a prominent part in the book. His brother John, then a senator, was also on the rackets committee, but Bobby was the culprit. An incredible story."

The priest said he never thought of Dave Beck these days without thinking about his feud with the IRS. "I have an opinion about that too," he said. "Looking back, I think he was the victim of a witchhunt instigated by Bobby Kennedy and Chairman McClellan. Jimmy Hoffa was a victim of the same harassment. Bobby, reportedly, had 75 IRS agents working on Hoffa to *get him*. Watergate was nothing, compared to Bobby Kennedy. That Dave Beck wouldn't *squeal* on Hoffa was to his credit, I think."

This, from a Catholic priest.

Dr. Charles P. Larson looked up from his coffee. The

internationally-known forensic pathologist had known
Dave Beck, he said, for nearly 40 years. He said he would
never forget a speech Dave made in Atlantic City in the
1950s. The occasion was an American Medical Association convention.

"It was one of the biggest crowds in AMA history,
about 17,000," Dr. Larson said. "Beck was the main
speaker. He gave a rousing speech—and without notes, too.
He just got up there at the podium and started swinging
away in typical Beck style—gesticulations, fist-pounding,
arms flailing the air, and that big, powerful voice. He had
17,000 doctors glued to their seats. Beck made me proud to
be from his state. He told that audience in no uncertain
terms that he was a staunch supporter of private enterprise and an opponent of socialized medicine. That was his
topic, socialized medicine. He said the AMA should be
trusted to police itself and that the government should
keep its nose out of it. As Dave talked, you could hear a pin
drop in that huge convention hall. Believe me, no one was
leaving early. And when he was finished, 17,000 doctors
rose to their feet and thundered applause on Dave for five
minutes.

"What made that response so damn significant was
that it came at a time when Beck was catching hell because
of the stand he was taking on socialized medicine. His picture was splashed all over the papers and some of the
things they were writing about him weren't precisely flat-
tering. To be perfectly blunt, Dave was highly suspect as a
labor leader, and a lot of those doctors went to hear Beck
with tongue in cheek. But it didn't take Dave long to fix
their wagons. I never saw anyone snickering when they left
the hall. Beck had completely made them believers."

The doctor paused. He sipped at his coffee.

"Listen," he said. "It took guts for Beck to say what he
said. That speech came at a time when the labor movement was very pro-socialized medicine. Yes, sir, he made
me very proud to be from the State of Washington."

Recently, I was sitting in a barber chair and two big

truck driver types walked into the shop and took their places in line. They were old customers. Frankie Gilletti, the barber, introduced us. "This is John McCallum," Frankie said. "He writes books. He's writing one right now on Dave Beck." They perked up.

"The old Teamsters boss?" one of them asked.

"The same."

"Best damned president we ever had," said the other. His partner nodded.

"Yes," he said. "I've been a Teamster for 37 years and say what you want about Beck, he did more for the union than anyone we ever had."

If Beck was still running things," the other said, "the Teamsters would be far more aggressive today."

Meeting Dave Beck for the first time, people are always a little startled by him, not only by his mild and self-effacing performance but by his personal appearance as well. His quiet, expensive clothes, his full-toothed smile, his bland face, his cordial handshake, give him the aura of a super Rotarian booster right out of *Main Street*. That's a natural impression, because he *is* a past District Deputy Grand Exalted Ruler of the northwest district of the Elks. He is also a 50-year honorary member of the American Legion—a former president of the Board of Regents of the University of Washington—and, ironically, considering the time he spent at McNeil Island, a one-time member of the Washington State Parole Board.

During the years 1952-1957 when he was riding high as president of the International Brotherhood of Teamsters, Warehousemen and Helpers of America, the biggest (1,584,00 members) and one of the richest and most powerful labor unions in the world, Beck was something of an enigma. He fit no previous pattern, considered from any point of view. He no more resembled the old craft-union leadership typified by such dinosaurs as Morris Hutchinson, Sr., of the Carpenters Union than he did the new politically-minded intellectually sophisticated leaders such as

Walter Reuther. In a good many ways, however, his career, his motivations, his methods, and his outlook on life were reminiscent of a breed that once freely roamed his part of the Pacific Northwest—empire builders like Stanford, Hill, and Weyerhaeuser, who, as much for the fun as for the money, rose by hook or crook to summits of personal power.

"Seattle had its rocky times. It was frontier country, the jumping-off place for the gold rush," Don Duncan said. "There's still a little bit of that around today. There's still some of that hey-let's-get-out-in-the-country-and-explore spirit; let's run up to Alaska, the ship's coming in."

Like the lumber barons, the cattle kings, and the mining magnates who had ruled the West before him, Beck saw the West as a vast, unfenced, unclaimed territory where a strong man could take what he wanted. Beck had wanted its roaming herds of labor. He rounded them up, hog-tied them, and branded them by the thousands. He fought off rustler Harry Bridges with one hand while piously rustling the herds of lesser unions with the other. Beck became something very unique in American labor: a regional prince whose power and interests extended far beyond the confines of labor and into the entire life of his community. Unlike Walter Reuther, Phil Murray, and John Lewis, he had no yearnings to become a political power or to take part in plotting a political labor party.

For years, Beck's principality stretched from Canada to Mexico, from the Rockies to the Pacific. The unions encompassed by his Western Conference of Teamsters moved virtually "everything on wheels" in the 11 western states. Later, as boss of the Teamsters, the world's largest single labor union, his round, pink face peered out of the cover of *Newsweek* under the bannerline: "This Man Can Make the U.S. Stand Still." His men sent enormous diesel rigs snarling down the Jersey Turnpike, drove hearses in Chicago, delivered laundry in Seattle, brought bread to the stores in Dallas, and unloaded mining machinery in Butte. Though truckers were the elite of the union, dozens of other oddly unrelated trades belonged too. They made beer, canned fruit, sold and serviced automobiles, pumped gasoline, worked in warehouses, and cleaned suits. They were undertakers, cow punchers, and aircraft mechanics.

Dave Beck not only dominated American labor in the 1950s, he dominated great chunks of business as well. He saw himself as a kind of self-appointed price-wage czar. With deadpan audacity he used his power to prevent cutthroat competition, to punish price cutters, and to help firms with Teamster contracts make a safe margin of profit. If some businessmen resented his interference, fear and respect prevented outcries. The sound of the name Dave Beck touched the nerve centers of thousands with the impact of a fist on bone. But the great majority of employers thought he was wonderful and applauded like happy seals when he addressed the Chamber of Commerce. They had their reasons: Beck abhorred strikes and stood for free enterprise with a capital E. He was an able, honest startlingly frank man, and in the latter years of his career, he became even startlingly reasonable. He was full of the kind of civic pride which rich industrialists had once reserved for themselves; he wanted his minions to prosper. His word and his contracts were as good as gold. He got porkchops for his unions but disciplined them with an iron hand.

In Seattle, where he has lived since he was four, Beck made himself a leading citizen. The job was done in part by the lever of power and the trowel of national publicity, but mostly by the touchstone of success. By virtue of his hard-won eminence, he rubbed shoulders with bankers and bishops; was close to Presidents Roosevelt, Truman, and Eisenhower; had private meetings with Sir Winston Churchill in London; raised funds for charity; served, beaming with pride, on various civic committees; and recently estimated that, over the years, personally attracted some $100 million in outside business to the City of Seattle. It was an exhilarating and heady experience for this man who once sold newspapers and Christmas trees and fished in houseboat-bordered Lake Union to help his parents keep the family together.

4
Off
and Running,
Mr. Beck

"HOW often do you go to see Beck?" a friend asked while I was researching and writing.

"At first, a couple times a week."

"How long at each session?"

"About four hours."

"Jesus, it must be great to sit there and listen in on a guy who made so much history. Jesus!" He had followed Beck's career for 30 years, he said. "You must be getting all this great stuff."

"Once he gets wound up, he can't stop."

"Well, that's the idea, isn't it? To get him to talk?"

Dave Beck and I were sitting in his apartment one morning, my tape cassette on my lap.

"Well," he said, addressing himself more to the microphone than to me, "where shall we begin?"

I looked at a long list of questions on my clipboard. "What about some general questions to warm up—what about giving some opinions of the Presidents you were close to? Roosevelt? Truman? Eisenhower?"

Beck settled himself in the chair opposite. He looked across at me and began to talk.

"I thought a great deal of Harry Truman," he said. "He was very human, very direct. He never beat around the bush, never double-talked you to death. You never had to try to figure out what was on his mind; he told you what was on his mind. Above all else, he was a man of his word. As much as I respected old Harry, I never had a disagreement with anybody in the President's office like I had with him. I never argued with him personally; rather, it was with Tom Clark, the attorney-general who later was named to the United States Supreme Court. We fought over the Hobbs Bill—Truman wanted to sign it; I was against it. We had a helluva fight over it. Afterwards in an attempt to heal the breach, Harry offered me the Secretary of Labor post, but I wouldn't think of it. I didn't want to be part of the Cabinet, I already had a good job—vice-president of the Teamsters. Anyway, Truman ignored my protests and went ahead and signed the Hobbs Bill—the most vicious anti-labor legislation the Teamsters have ever been confronted with.

"Roosevelt? I have mixed emotions about FDR. Personally, I had a lot of confidence in his ability. I think he was the ideal man for the job at that particular time in our history. In my opinion, he was the *only* man in our whole country who could have done the job he did. And yet, everything had to fall in place for him to do it. Industry was desperate; the banks were going broke. There wasn't a bank in the U.S.A. that didn't fight the deposit law; today, that's the last thing in the world they'd give up. Yet, I know individuals—I know positively—that Roosevelt called in for help; he promised them certain appointments and then walked right away from them. So the bottom line on Roosevelt was this: *I don't think his word was worth a damn!*

"As for Eisenhower, he just didn't know what it was all about; the Presidency, I mean. Poor Ike didn't have any training for the job. Oh, he was a highclass, decent individual, but he was just out of his class in big-time politics."

I stirred. In 1959, I wrote a book titled *Six Roads From Abilene*, the story of the Eisenhowers. I spent hours at a time with Edgar Eisenhower, the President's brother. During the Eisenhower years I saw much of the Presidency through family eyes. I told Beck how angry Edgar would get whenever he saw in the papers how Truman was attacking brother Ike. Old Harry once accused Ike of having a swelled head. "You'd think," Truman said, "that a fellow who comes from Kansas, where all the folks are just plain folks, wouldn't let his success as a professional military man go to his head some way or other. I don't know what causes it. It's just too bad." I thought Edgar Eisenhower was going to have a coronary then and there.

Beck smiled, all teeth.

"The irony," he said, "is that Truman and Ike's oldest brother, Arthur, once shared a room together. They lived in a place called Mrs. Trow's boardinghouse, in Kansas City, and had jobs in banks. Harry and Art got along fine."

I said, "That's one for history. Two roommates: one becomes President of the United States on the Democratic ticket, and the other's brother gets elected President on the Republican ticket. Small world."

Beck appeared thoughtful. "I never did know what Truman had against Ike. Something happened to split them."

"Old Harry hurt Ike terribly," I said. "When the dedication of the Truman Library was held at Independence, Ike was there. A few years later, when it came time for the dedication of the Eisenhower Library at Abilene, Truman didn't come. He was less than a hundred miles away, yet he failed to repay the courtesy. Ike took it pretty hard, Edgar Eisenhower told me."

I then asked Beck to try to recall the very first time he talked to Sir Winston Churchill.

"It was in London," he said. "I was there to address the British Trade Union Congress as a delegate from the American Federation of Labor. I met him again in Miami Beach, Florida, at a social affair hosted by Mr. Clark, the

Canadian railroad tycoon. On a Sunday night Mr. Clark gave this private dinner in honor of Churchill, and I went with a party of 60 people. The third time I met him was in London again. We had a long talk on questions and issues of interest to England and the United States. I was always opposed to the labor movement becoming a political organization. I've always advocated that it should be an economic organization. In my opinion it was drifting far from that in England. 'But that is the right of the British labor movement to choose for themselves,' I told the Prime Minister. 'Just as it is the right of the Russians to choose any form of government they elect. The only promise I ask from them in return is that they allow us to live the way we want to live, without any outside pressures from communism, etcetera. Nor do we, the United States, have the right to tell the British government, or the Russian government, or the Germans, or anybody else how they should live as it relates to their domestic, inside affairs. That's their own right.' Those were the issues that Mr. Churchill and I talked about.

"I was very impressed with Mr. Churchill. He was an excellent listener—seemed totally interested in my views. He had absolutely fantastic mental power and superb constitutional energy. When he made a decision, he stuck to his guns no matter the consequences. He also had marvelous vision; in fact, when it came to the question of Russia, he showed better vision than Roosevelt. Above all, Mr. Churchill was a great orator. I heard him make that historic speech before the U.S. Congress soon after we entered World War II.

"Mr. Churchill once was asked to address the students at his old prep school. He got up before them, shook a fist at 'em, and in that low, thundering voice, boomed: 'NEVER GIVE UP—NEVER, NEVER, NEVER!' That's all he said. Then he sat down. There was nothing more essential he could tell them. He had said it all."

I said, "You told Churchill that labor should not get involved in politics."

He made a rumbling, keening sound in this throat.

"I never made that statement. I told Churchill that, in my opinion, the solution to the problems of labor was *not* political action. Granted, we must keep a hand in politics, because we have matters before the state legislature, the city council, the county government, and the national Congress, but we have to build the structure of labor on *economics*. What they give you today they can take away from you tomorrow in political action. What you accomplish by economic action, nobody's going to take away from you if you continue to build and strengthen your position. That's the vast difference between the British Trade Movement and the American Labor Movement. One is political, the other is economic.

"I'll give you an illustration. I can name right now, in the Teamsters, five people who were given brand new automobiles of their choices when they retired recently. As mementos of their long services to the union, they were told they could pick the model. So what did they pick? A Ford? A Chevrolet? A Plymouth? A Lincoln? No—they *all* got European cars. Now, the whole printing trade of America has been built around the union label in printing; the garment industry of America revolves around the fight of its life to organize the largest manufacturer of garment material in the country. Now, show me where you've got a union label on a foreign car. Yet, here were five leading Teamsters who, secretly or otherwise, said to the union, 'Well, if you're going to give me an automobile for a going-away present, make it a Mercedes-Benz.' Sure, I understand the balance of trade issue and all those details. I can appreciate why we have to have foreign commerce. But those people, earning their living in the labor movement, are thoughtless and just plain crazy when they shun our American products for something foreign. They wouldn't have done it if they'd stopped and thought about it. 'You're certainly not going to buy a foreign car with thousands of Americans out of work, are you?' Such a question would have had them stumbling around to find an answer."

I went on, "I'm going to throw some names at you. Tell me what immediately pops into your mind."

Beck nodded his head.

"First," I said, "John L. Lewis."

"John L. had more ability than anyone I've ever met in the American Labor Movement. Outstanding ability, a great orator, a man with vast experience and ability consummating law in the legislative field, a tremendous organizer and leader. I doubt if ever we will see his equal again."

"Your old adversary—Harry Bridges."

"A tremendous organizer. While I couldn't accept his political philosophy, I agreed with him overwhelmingly when it came to economic action. Bridges had an uncanny ability to recognize the physical picture he operated in. He utilized every single avenue open to him, and he made giant progress for his union by building a close working relationship between the longshoremen and the maritime organizations."

"Walter Reuther."

"A good student, one with a tendency to lean toward a straight line. Communism? I don't know. I know something inspired him and his brother to go to Russia and work there; whatever it was should have qualified him to show the weaknesses of the Russian system as opposed to our way—as well as the strengths. I think Reuther took advantage, to the nth degree, of the huge membership he had in a certain small locale of our population generally. He moved in and took over in contradiction to the courts. They made it virtually impossible for the law to stop them. They simply went into Detroit, seized the auto factories, and sat there refusing to budge. You couldn't have blown 'em out with a howitzer. That's how Reuther actually organized the atomotive industry. And that, of course, was his great objective and the backbone of the union. Yet Reuther criticized the militancy of the Teamsters."

"George Meany."

"At first, Meany and I were friends. I don't think we were bosom friends; time has demonstrated we were not. John L. Lewis and I were very good friends. All during the years I was in Washington, D.C., as president of the Teamsters, John L. and I ate lunch together several times a week if he was in town. We always ate at a hotel located across the street from the Statler. I never was a good friend of Bridges. Bridges and I came in conflict in the field of jurisdiction. We fought over the issue of the warehouse-men on the docks and back of the waterfront; we fought again when war broke out over the cannery workers. So there was never a close relationship with Bridges. Further-more, I objected vigorously to his alleged ties with com-munism. Politically, he was not a man I wanted to be asso-ciated with.

"I was never close to Reuther, either. I'm not saying he was jealous, but I think he got his nose out of joint when the Teamsters grew past the United Automobile Workers, which was supposed to be the biggest labor union in the world. And I kept rubbing it in. I kept reminding Reuther that we were only getting started, that 'you ain't seen nothin' yet.' Like Topsy, we jes' grew and grew. I could hear Reuther grumbling all the way back to Seattle. I think he got just plain jealous of our progress. Then, of course, adding fuel to the fire between the Teamsters and the UAW was the fact that we didn't sit in his corner during his battle with the A.F.ofL. Frankly, we sided with the Amer-ican Federation of Labor, giving it whatever financial and economic strength we had. We were with them every inch of the way."

"John F. Kennedy."

"In my opinion, he showed uncommonly good ability

as a President. But I don't think he'll be remembered in history as a *great* President. He displayed terribly poor judgment in Cuba—the Bay of Pigs decision. I think, however, he did some things which should be applauded; he was loyal, for example, to the principles of the labor movement. He was a friend of labor. In that regard brother Bobby even measured up. Bobby's problem was that he was so damned ambitious. He didn't hesitate a minute to move into New York and run against a fine senator with an excellent prolabor voting record and defeat him there. Why? Because it was in Bobby's selfish interests to do it."

"Do you still hold any bitterness against Bobby Kennedy?" I asked.

"Somebody asked me the other day if I'd make any comments about the Kennedys," he said. "I said I certainly would. I said, 'Let's start with Teddy Kennedy and Chappaquiddick. If you're ready to start there, I'm ready to tell you anything you want to know.' And right away the subject was dropped. There is no family in the history of America with a more inconsistent political background than Kennedys. Joe Kennedy, the old man! He was everything your teacher said you shouldn't be. I liked John, the President, better than any of 'em. But nobody who was ever President of the United States, and while he was in the Senate, was rumored to be a bigger playboy than John Kennedy."

As a fist flew out to punctuate a point, I changed the subject. Dave Beck was about to boil over.

"Senator Joe McCarthy," I said.

"A damn fool," Beck said. "Simply a stupid ass. He isn't worthy of more than that in this book. The sonuvabitch almost ruined the country! Thank God, we survived that terrible period. But he did serve to make one important point—we must develop a society and a governmental structure that'll allow people to express themselves freely, whether it's acceptable to us or whether we applaud it or would destroy it. We still cannot interfere with the right of freedom of speech, whether it be via TV, radio, newspapers, or the picket signs. We must maintain the right to express ourselves."

I said, "Jimmy Hoffa once boasted that everybody feared the Teamsters. The image that people had of him was that he was tough."

"Jimmy's philosophy was—be tougher than the other guy," Beck explained.

"Hoffa was a man on the move," I said. "Did you ever have the feeling he was after your job?"

"Around 1947," Beck answered, "Dan Tobin wanted to put Hoffa on the General Executive Board. I was summoned to Toronto to confer with Tobin. He wanted me, as a member of the Teamsters Board, to approve his putting Hoffa in a vacancy on the board. I told Tobin, 'I won't vote for Hoffa. That appointment belongs in the West, not the East.' The Western Conference of Teamsters comprised a third of the union's total membership. I said, 'I won't vote for anybody unless he's a Westerner.' I don't remember whether I recommended Chicago's Bill Lee or Seattle's Frank Brewster, but it was one of them, anyway. Chicago wasn't in the Western Conference, but at least it was west of the East. The Western Conference took in 11 states, Hawaii, and British Columbia. I said to Tobin, 'Go ahead and pick Hoffa. You've got the power to do it, but I'm not voting for him.' Tobin said, 'Well, I won't do it unless you approve and it's unanimous.'"

"What happened then?" I asked.

"I went downstairs, where I bumped into Hoffa and invited him to have lunch with me," Beck said. "He had already eaten, so we had a cup of coffee. I didn't beat around the bush. I came right out and told him I wouldn't vote for him. I said, 'I have nothing personal against you, Jimmy; you've done an excellent job as an organizer, but that seat on the board belongs in the West.' He was disappointed, but brightened when I added, 'In about nine months there's a convention in Los Angeles and we're adding two new board members. If you're a candidate, I'll vote for you then.' And that's what happened. When we met at L.A., Hoffa was elected to the board.

"After that, Tobin retired, and I moved up to president of the Teamsters. Hoffa was now vice-president and was head of the local organization in Detroit. As a vice-president he sat on the executive board, and he worked under my direction on various assignments I delegated to him. Actually, I got along with Hoffa fine. We never had any disagreements. He was not responsible for any administrative duties; he was not on a salary of the International Union. Hoffa simply attended board meetings every three months. There the policy of the union was enunciated until the next conference, and he got to vote on that."

"You must have had a personal opinion of Jimmy Hoffa," I said. "To the vast public, he was something of an enigma."

"Hoffa was one of the ablest organizers in the history of the trade union movement," Beck said. "I mean, you can go back as far as 1926 and you won't find any better. Of all the labor organizers I've ever met—and I have known 98 per cent of all the outstanding leaders of the American labor movement, from John L. Lewis to George Meany—I would have to place Jimmy Hoffa right up there near No. 1."

"How well did you know Hoffa? I mean, the *real* Jimmy Hoffa," I said.

"I probably knew him as well as anyone—which probably isn't saying much."

"But you must have gotten pretty close to him."

"Professionally, yes; socially, no," Beck explained. "I had very little social relationship with him. To the best of my recollection, in all the years we worked together—he in Detroit and me in Seattle—at best we were only semi-close. Even after I became president, he still worked out of Detroit and I was headquartered in Washington. Believe this, in all those years the Hoffas and the Becks never sat down to dinner together. There simply was no social relationship, family or otherwise. I love sports, but I never attended a sporting event with Hoffa either. So if there was another side of him besides what the public saw, I never saw it. What I saw was his working side. He was a very hard worker. Tough? Sure, he was tough. He went out to organize, and he did an organizer's job. He faced the roughest, toughest people, and he fought them on equal ground. His motto seemed to be: 'Do unto others—*first.*' But, hell, anybody who's ever read history in school knows that the labor movement evolved out of force—violence. Go back 100 years, 200 years, there have been 10,000 fights. Miners, lumberjacks, auto builders, newspapermen—where have we had more vicious fights than in the circulation wars in New York and Chicago? So when you say Hoffa was tough and rough, that's the way you had to be in the 1930s and 1940s to survive. People fought to protect themselves. The blacks did it in the South to stop lynching. The Irish, Italians, Poles, the Jews—they all came out fighting to earn self-respect and a place in our society. Hell, America was born out of revolution. Sure, the labor movement was part of it. I don't deny for one second there was vicious fighting in order for labor to win the right to conduct itself under the process of collective bargaining. It's a big subject—an historic subject—but Jimmy Hoffa adjusted himself to whatever was necessary to get the job done.

"Hoffa was a tireless worker. He worked day and night, Sundays and holidays. He dedicated himself to the Teamsters and the cause of labor. If he made a mistake—the misappropriation of union finances, for example—I'm not here to say, because I don't know. I do know that he was employed primarily to improve wages and working conditions for the Teamsters, and he lay awake nights struggling for a solution. Then he worked all day trying to put his aims into effect. So when you're judging Jimmy Hoffa, give him a break; be charitable, at least for what he did for the Teamsters. He demonstrated a hundred per cent he was qualified for the job—and he earned his salary."

"A great mystery still surrounds the disappearance of Hoffa. Surely, you must have an opinion of what happened to him," I said.

"When Hoffa first came out of prison, I advised him to stay in retirement," Beck said. "I could see, from reading the papers and talking to different people, that an internal struggle was developing within the Teamsters. I felt Hoffa had everything to lose and little to gain by trying to regain the presidency. And the Teamsters had everything to gain, and little to lose, by allowing Hoffa to give whatever help and support he could to Fitzsimmons, who, in my opinion, had effected a miracle by helping him get out of prison. How Fitz did it, what strings he pulled, was beside the point; the fact remained that Hoffa got out of jail. In my judgment that should have been paramount. Hoffa should have forgotten about coming back to the Teamsters, except to give any aid and assistance he could, the same as I was doing. I advised Hoffa not to make a personal issue out of the presidency. I told him, 'Forget about going back into office. It'll do nothing but provoke an internal fight within the union; your persistence is only going to hurt the membership and everybody else connected with the Teamsters.' The big issue, I think, was whether or not Hoffa had the right to seek another term as president after he got back from prison. Fitzsimmons said he did not, that's all I know."

I said, "There have been many theories as to why Hoffa was killed. Some say it involved the manner in which Teamster money was being invested; that Hoffa was going to name names. *Big* names."

"I heard the same rumors," Beck said. "Hoffa had been making some pretty bold statements. Whether fact or fiction, he claimed there were some unqualified investment people squandering Teamster pension funds. He threatened to expose those people. His position couldn't lead to anything but trouble. I don't know who could fear what he had to say enough to have him killed—except someone, perhaps, who was a party to finders' fees or some such who were associated with loans that created great losses."

"Recently, I met Dr. John F. Burton," I said. "he was the Chief Deputy Medical Examiner of Detroit and the County of Oakland, Michigan. He was the first black forensic pathologist in the United States—the *only* one in the country's history. Since Hoffa disappeared in his jurisdiction, it was Dr. Burton's responsibility to try to find the body. Dr. Burton told me it was the most baffling case he'd ever had. He said he got a call one night saying Hoffa had vanished and for him to be prepared. So he telegraphed five consultants and specialists. He advised them to be ready to begin the search. He said he got them all alerted—got their plane fares ready—and then *nothing*. 'What happened?' I asked Dr. Burton, waiting for a punch line. 'Nothing,' he said. 'That's the end of the story.' And I said, 'You mean, you never even looked for Hoffa?' 'Oh, we tried to find him, all right,' he said. 'We spent thousands of dollars digging, scraping, and excavating around his neighborhood in Pontiac, looking for the body, but we got nowhere. Zilch. Finally, after a week, everybody packed up and went home. That, sir, ended the search for Jimmy Hoffa. Damnedest case I've ever known. His tracks ended at a restaurant. From there he just disappeared in thin air. Those people play rough. Everytime I turned around, somebody from the Hoffa bunch was missing. He had a lot of enemies.'"

I looked straight at Beck. "Dave," I asked, "do you have any ideas where Hoffa is?"

"I don't know," he said. "But wherever he is, he ain't talking."

5

Turn Back the Clock

TURN BACK the clock to the Gaslight Era in America and the effect is curious. Historians lyrically refer to it as the "good old days," an age when fashion featured the Gibson girl look, with hoop skirts and bustles, and tiny waists, while styles for men dictated the handlebar mustache, slick-parted hair, high-buttoned jacket, and tall stiff collar. It was a time when Dad rode Mom on a bicycle built for two, and when two could live as cheaply as one without both working.

It was also an era of change. Out at Wounded Knee Creek, South Dakota, the Seventh Cavalry was bringing to a close gory, pitched battles between Indians and horse soldiers by slaughtering 200 redskins in the Army's revenge for the massacre of General Custer. It was a time of the first major industrial strike in the country's history, one which shut down the Carnegie Steel empire; a time when Benjamin Harrison was finishing his term as President, while Grover Cleveland, William McKinley, and Teddy Roosevelt warmed up in the bullpen.

The Gaslight Era, the Gay Nineties, the Good Old Days—call it what you will—but a tourist's view of the times would indicate that there were troubles too. Between the years 1889 and 1906 Johnstown, Pennsylvania, suffered a disastrous flood, Chicago an incredible fire, and San Francisco a devastating earthquake. Holocausts to be sure, but life went on. The Duryea, a four-horsepower automobile, one of the first, made its appearance. Edison built his Kinetographic Theatre, the first movie studio. Vaudeville flourished. Buffalo Bill Cody, the western hero of the period, toured the national theater circuit. Joseph Jefferson III enthralled audiences with his characterization of Rip Van Winkle. Millions flocked to the Chicago World's Fair of 1893.

On the international scene the United States was forced to send relief corps to the Far East to suppress the bloody Boxer Rebellion in China. The *Maine*, American battleship, was blown up in Havana Harbor, killing 260 men and touching off the Spanish-American war. Teddy Roosevelt led a charge of his Rough Riders up San Juan Hill in Cuba. He won the Nobel Prize for settling the war in 1905 between Russian and Japanese troops. Four years before that, on September 6, 1901, Leon Czolgosz, a young anarchist, shocked the world by assassinating President McKinley at Buffalo's Pan-American Exposition. Roosevelt succeeded the slain President.

On December 17, 1903, the Wright brothers made the first successful airplane flight at Kitty Hawk, North Carolina. John D. Rockefeller struck oil, amassed a fortune of more than $300,000,000 at the turn of the century. Edison's movie of "The Great Train Robbery" was the first film to tell a story.

In sports, world heavyweight champion John L. Sullivan went around shouting, "I can lick any so-and-so in the house!" Most of the time he was right—until, on September 7, 1892, in New Orleans, Gentleman Jim Corbett knocked him out in 21 rounds. It was the first heavyweight championship prizefight in history in which the combatants wore gloves. The diversity among pugilists added tremendous spice and drama to the sport—the flamboyant John L., the clever Gentleman Jim, the sullen Jim Jeffries, the shuffling Bob Fitzsimmons, the intemperate Stanley Ketchel.

Sports had advanced remarkably since the Civil War, but we were only emerging from swaddling clothes. Basketball was just eight years old in 1900; most speed swimmers used the sidestroke; track athletes won Olympic titles in times that schoolboys would scoff at today; and horse racing was about to see a reform wave which would close every track except those in Kentucky and Maryland. Football, still dominated by Yale, Harvard, and Princeton, was a push-and-pull business based on power and brawn. Baseball was still creaking along on legs as unsteady as a new-born colt's. Fans rode to the ball parks in horse-drawn buses. John J. McGraw was then a 5'-6", 121-pound third baseman, the brain and sparkplug of the championship Baltimore Orioles, considered by some to be the greatest ball club of all time. These were the early days, when a ball park was a rough, uncultivated lot, a grandstand was a jumble of rickety slats, and a club payroll looked like the wage list of a logging camp. A French-Canadian hack driver, Larry Lajoie, was the sensation of the new American League. He was such an idol that the crowds followed him down the streets, and kids worshipped him. When he endorsed a certain brand of chewing tobacco, half the kids of the nation got sick giving the foul weed a trial in the hope it would make them sluggers too.

It was in those times that Dave Beck was born and spent his boyhood.

Lemuel Beck, Dave's father, was a native of Tennessee. As a young man he came out to California. He had no special trade but became an auctioneer in the greater San Francisco area, where he met and married Mary Tierney, a local girl. It was Lemuel's second marriage, Mary's first. He had a son, Victor, by his first wife. Because he left home early and went out on his own, Victor and Dave were never very close; they saw little of each other as grown men. Victor settled down in South Tacoma, where he worked as a night watchman for the Northern Pacific Railroad. Frank Gilletti was his barber.

"From the mouth up, Vic and Dave Beck looked a lot alike," Frankie told me. "But from the shoulders down Vic was not as husky as Dave. His moods were change-able—feisty one moment, low-key the next. Like his younger half-brother, he could be very explosive when provoked, a real scrapper. Yet he could be very gentle, too—like Dave. Everybody liked Vic. He was a good story-teller. He'd sit in my barber chair and talk a foot off about experiences that happened to him on the job. Once, he said, he surprised a young kid who was robbing the N.P.R. office. When the kid looked up and saw him, he made a dash for the door. Vic shouted at him to stop, or he'd shoot. The kid kept going, so Vic shot him in the butt. Later, after the kid got out of the hospital, he was put on probation by a sympathetic judge. The first thing the kid did was to come back and thank Vic for shooting him in the pants. He told Vic, "I'm going straight now. That bullet in the ass was just what I needed. I'm never going to get into trouble again.' And he didn't.

"Victor Beck was a strong Mormon. He never drank coffee, boozed, or smoked. He lived to 86; died of cancer in 1974."

Dave Beck recalls:

"Our father was either English or German, I don't remember which. He died in 1924, when I was about 30. After my parents married, they settled for a while in Stockton, California. That's where I was born, on June 16, 1894, followed by my sister, Reta, 16 months later. When I was about two, our father went up to Seattle to establish a

business. Mom, Reta, and I joined him two years later. By
the time we joined him, he was running a carpet shop down
on Third Avenue, between Seneca and Spring streets. In
those days, the entire city revolved around Pike Street.

"We journeyed from California on the *Walla Walla*, in
steerage. There was little money, and we were forced to
travel under the most rigid of conditions. The *Walla Walla*
was one of the boats with the *Umatilla* and the *Pueblo* that
were the main artery of traffic between Seattle, San Francisco,
and Los Angeles. I was four years old. Father was operating
this carpet shop, laying carpets, repairing them, fixing furniture—that sort of thing. He was a hard worker, a robust,
aggressive man who stood 5'-10" and weighed 240 pounds,
terribly overweight. I resemble my dad in a lot of ways,
even to an identical baldness. The exception was business
judgment. We were always poor—very, very poor. If it
hadn't been for mother handling what money there was,
our family would have starved. But dad was a wonderful
man in other ways. They say that the best headstart a boy
can get in life is a father he can respect and care for.
Almost all villains in history, big or small, lacked such a
model from their early years on—Caesar, Nero, and
Hitler—they all were deprived of such father-figures. Well,
I loved and respected my father.

"Once an auctioneer, he was a very fine speaker and a
sound thinker. He handled himself aptly in front of an
audience—had a good speaking voice, a grasp for words.
He was an inveterate reader and encouraged me to read
books. I have been a book-reader all my life—biography,
mostly, about successful men.

"Our first home in Seattle was in the Belltown district. Denny School was my first grammar school. You're a
genuine oldtimer, a pioneer, if you remember Denny,
because it was torn down years ago to make way for a
regrade project.

"I was nine years old when we moved from Belltown to
815 Pike Street, where we lived in the backend of dad's

carpet shop. It was cheaper, combining the working and living quarters. We simply partitioned the two sections with a draw curtain.

"Thinking about my boyhood, one memory stands out particularly. In the summer of my ninth birthday, Mom, Reta, and I traveled in steerage again down to San Francisco to visit her father, who had been very ill. That August (the 14th, to be specific), my uncle, mom's brother, took me to my first prizefight—and what a fight. Jim Jeffries, the world heavyweight champion, defended his title against the former champ, James J. Corbett. The thing that made the match so interesting was that Jeffries once had been Corbett's sparring partner. There aren't many of us left who saw the Jeffries-Corbett fight, but I did."

The event Beck refers to was the *second* fight between Jeffries and Corbett. An earlier match was held on May 11, 1900, at Coney Island, New York, and Jeffries won on a knockout in the 23rd round.

By 1903, Gentleman Jim was regarded by the experts as a has-been. He had been living a fast life. He ran a thriving saloon on Broadway, between 33rd and 34th streets in Manhattan. The intrigue began when he came to Billy Brady, his old manager who had hitched himself to Jeff's star and made him champion, and told him a tale of debts and need and begged him to give him another match with his former sparring partner. Out of pity and for auld lang syne, Brady signed him on. San Francisco was picked as the logical site for the bout because both Corbett and Jeffries were from California.

Outside San Francisco's old Yosemite Atheltic Club, where the bout was fought, Dave remembers still the dark crush of men, and men only. These sports in checked suits or dark, heavy fustian with the ubiquitous bowler or hard hat atop their heads moved in a steady, steamy crush toward the entrances, breathing fight talk and alcohol fumes, to the brassy cries of the ticket speculators, leather-lunged scamps in high silk hats with paper money bent around the fingers of both hands.

Inside the Yosemite Athletic Club a vast, gas-lit arena, Dave peered through a blue fog of smoke from five-cent "cee-gars." Every man of the audience appeared to have a cigar in his red face. Men and men only. Women were not allowed into this purely masculine paradise.

The prize ring was in the center beneath a battery of sputtering arc lights, installed because of those new-fangled motion picture cameras. Yosemite Athletic Club was quivering with lust and excitement. It would be hard for modern fight fans to picture how brutal, how mean and stone-hard was that San Francisco audience the night Jeffries fought Corbett in defense of his world championship. San Francisco was yet a growing city, and its dregs went to a prize fight. One and all they were men who preyed on other men in one way or another. The roar of that mob echoed a coarseness and obscenity.

They came at last, the two fighters followed by their entourages, managers, seconds, handlers, bucket-carriers, bottle-holders, towel-swingers, as big and burly and hard-bitten a crew as ever climbed out of the sinks of society. Jeffries was clad in trousers, red sweater, and cap pulled down over his big, surly head. Corbett was dressed more elegantly. In those days they wore their knee-length, woolen fighting trunks fastened at the waist with an American flag beneath their street clothes and stripped in the ring before the eyes of the crowd.

A sigh went up as Corbett peeled down for action. By jingoes, he was in shape. A slender stripling compared to the brawny, hairy former boilermaker Jeffries, who was taller and 45 pounds heavier.

How simple in those days. No boxing commission, no inspectors, no examining physicians, nothing but a pair of powerful, tough guys, many of whom made up their rules as they went along. The gloves were finally produced. They weighed four ounces.

The referee was Ed Graney, in shirt sleeves with armlets and braces, topped off by a handlebar mustache. There were no judges. Ed Graney had absolute power. He could award the fight to one or the other, call it a draw, call bets off on a foul, or throw them both out of the ring.

Beck's eyes sparkled as he continued. "Even though it was 75 years ago, I remember there were no instructions from the referee. The ring was cleared, the two fighters stood alone in their corners. The clang of the bell was heard. Jeffries and Corbett moved toward the center of the ring, shook hands, and the battle was on.

"While it took 23 rounds for Big Jeff to flatten Corbett the first time they fought, this time he did it in 10. By now the champion had acquired the polish and skill which only experience could give him, while Corbett was feeling his 36 years. In the tenth round, Jeff stood straight up and rushed out of his corner at Jim. Corbett seemed to be making a waiting fight. They exchanged lefts to the face, with Jeff making a vicious effort to end the fight with one punch. Then Jeff sent a left hook to the stomach, and Corbett dropped to the canvas for a count of nine. He got up and Jeff was all over him, smothering him with another left to the belly and a powerful right to the jaw. Corbett went down again, and when the count reached seven, his corner tossed in the sponge. Corbett was in terrible pain. A chair was brought for him. After a minute's rest he recovered, got up, and shook hands with Jeff.

"Corbett had one weakness as a fighter. He lacked the killer instinct. He loved to box, but there was nothing really brutal about him. He was fast physically and mentally, yet slow and deliberate in his speech. In and out of the prize ring he was always a great actor. As a matter of fact, he later became an actor on the Broadway stage.

"Boxing is the oldest of human sports. It appeals to the primitive instincts of man. Beneath this veneer is the cave man, the man of violence and aggression. Few sports rely so heavily on personalities as boxing. As a one-time member of the Seattle Boxing Commission, when prize-fighting rode high in the Pacific Northwest, I knew a lot of the champions: Jimmy McLarnin, Freddie Steele, Al Hostak, and Jack Dempsey to name only a few. They taught me that boxing is a great leveler. Like myself, they demonstrated that wealth, education, inherited privilege, and superficial cleverness are unimportant. It's what is in your heart that counts."

I suppose oldtimers are the same everywhere. Because they've survived the past, they love it, and because they're not at all certain they'll survive the present, they hate it. To most of them, the world was indeed a better place when they were young. I say "most" because Dave Beck is not one who would want to go back. He remembers the "Good Ol' Days" as a time of luck and pluck. He remembers it as a time of hunger, hard work, an uncertain future. He remembers Christmas as a time when his family was "too poor to give gifts," and Thanksgiving as a day without the traditional family dinner. Summer vacations from school were not vacations at all. "We always worked—there was no time for a real vacation," Beck remembers.

But maybe I'm making it sound more dismal than it really was. He had fun. Sure, he did. What, for example, did he do on Halloween? "Anything we could get away with," he laughed. It was a time to howl, to rage, to scream, to raise the dead and stun the living, long into the dark October night and beyond. It was a time for raising hackles and gooseflesh; a time for every block in Seattle to become its own Bald Mountain, as young Dave and his companions were turned loose. God help Old Sour Puss down the block who wouldn't let Dave get his football out of his shrubs, or the fruit store proprietor who wouldn't allow any of the guys to swipe an apple from time to time, or the truant officer who made them go to school. And God help anyone who hadn't the good sense to strap down everything removable. For 364 days of the year Dave and his chums obeyed the rules, more or less; but on Halloween, they were footloose and the city was theirs.

A strange light comes into Beck's eyes when he talks about the things he did when he was a kid. The ice wagon on the roof of the bandstand cupola down in the park—how did it get there? A back-breaking job for a dozen workmen with a crane, impossible for kids. But there it would be the next morning for a rising Seattle to look upon and wonder, all aghast. Perhaps the Seven Wonders of the World were so created.

There were also privies to be overturned, windows to be soaped and waxed, horses to be painted. They would roam the streets with ticktacks, those notched empty spools with the wind-up string that made such an ear-splitting racket when run against windows; or with the open-end tin cans and resined cord attachments, excellent for waking Old Grouch; or with scraped-out pumpkins.

But over to Old Sour Puss's house for the best prank of all. Dave and six masked genies creeping stealthily up the front porch steps, silent as ghosts, carrying a sack of light-bulbs. Ring the doorbell; wait.

"Yes? Who is it?" calls out Old Sour Puss.

Select the biggest lightbulbs in the sack.

"Who is it, please?"

Start dropping the bulbs onto the echoing porch floors.

"Don't do it, Butch, don't kill me!" *Pow!* "I didn't squeal to the cops on ya!" *Pow!* "Please—somebody help me!" *Pow!* "Ya got me!" *Pow, pow, pow!* Giggles, howls, a parting obscenity, and run like the devil!

Compare those times with today's jack-o'-lanterns, corn-silk mustaches, old sheets and hooded masks, and the trick-or-treat bags. Tell the toddlers that you choose to be tricked and they are thrown into confusion. Conformity has dulled the edge of what was once a grand old sport.

"The fate of the Fourth of July is no less sobering," Beck recalls. "What started out in 1776 as a unique and stirring day of commemoration, completely American in origin and observance, has declined to just another day off the job, or out of school, a chance to watch a doubleheader between the Seattle Mariners and Oakland in the after-noon and a few fireworks at night. Where are the brass bands and parades, the patriotic, flamboyant speeches, the picnics, the gunnysack races, the tug-o'-wars, the first fried chicken of the year, and the best ice cream (homemade) that ever was? And, of course, the fireworks. In our day, *Chinese* firecrackers. With them you could make the loudest bangs ever heard. You could feel the independence right down to your toes—the same sort of independence that must have stirred the men of the Continental Army. When those Chinese ten-inchers exploded, they sounded just like the skirmishing of muskets.

"Oh, the Fourth of July used to be a grand old day, an exciting, noisy, wonderful day.

"Exciting?" the kids ask today. "What did you do?"

"Well, you touched a punk to a flashcracker and tossed it into a sewer, then waited for the boom that echoed all the way up and down the line. You placed torpedoes on the streetcar tracks—how do you describe the startled look on the face of the motorman when he ran over them? You hurled cherry bombs—glittery red grenades—that exploded on contact with, let us say, a passing coal truck. And you lighted firecrackers underneath cans and you ran a few steps and turned and watched the cans fly up. You buried firecrackers up to their fuses in dirt and set them off.

"Didn't you get dirty?"

"Very."

"What else?"

"Well, you held ladyfingers in your hand and, with great daring, lighted them; and they would begin to sizzle, but you held on—"

"Didn't they go off in your hand?"

"Sure, but they didn't hurt, if you knew how to hold them: loosely, at the very ends.

"We shot off rockets, of course. There were a few homemade rockets, and plenty of ways of sending them off. Rainspouts were preferred, and a six-foot drainpipe was a thing to treasure all year as the ideal Fourth of July launching pad. You could buy two rockets for as little as four pennies. But it was the Chinese firecrackers that we loved best. They came wrapped up in an odd, crinkly, wax-colored paper, usually with funny drawings of American kids with Oriental eyes. They came in all different sizes, "one-inchers to ten-inchers."

"Weren't they dangerous?"

"Sure, but that was part of the thrill."

"They're against the law now."

"When I was a kid, they were legal. Every kid with the tiniest bit of common sense knew enough to leave a dud alone and to get out of the way of a homemade rocket when it was being launched. True, there were accidents, injuries, even deaths, but they were just a fraction compared with today—mostly the result of auto accidents, going to and from beaches and campgrounds. After a long, full day of firecrackers, pinwheels, rockets, and the whole gamut of noisemakers, we'd crawl into bed at night, dirty, exhausted, sometimes bandaged and blistered; and we got up the next morning miraculously free of frustrations, satisfied with ourselves, ready to cope with the problems of our gray little worlds.

"We might have won the American Revolution, but it appears that big segments of the spirit of the Continental troops have been lost. Very little remains of what once was the Grand and Glorious Fourth: here and there an American flag, the occasional distant thud of a smuggled cherry bomb, but mostly quiet streets, deserted cities, a few family picnics, a band concert or two, and a total absence of pageantry. *The kids are being robbed!*"

Dave Beck makes no secret of the fact that he was raised in poverty in a ramshackle house in Seattle's old Belltown near the south end of Lake Union.

"We were poor as hell," he says. One way he helped out was to sell newspapers, catch fish and sell them, and he sold fir trees at Christmas. "Sometimes," he remembers, "my father and I fished in Lake Union for something to eat that day."

Another way Dave helped out was to roam under the

wharves of Lake Union with a borrowed .22 rifle, shooting rats.

"In those days," Beck said, "Seattle was on guard against signs of the bubonic plague brought in by rats from ships out of the Orient. When I got a sack full of rats, I'd take them up to the Health Department. They would nail them on wooden slabs and cut them open. For every rat which showed signs of the plague, I got $5.00. If my mother had ever found out I was carrying around sacks of dead rats, she would have slapped me good, so I told her I made money running errands or helping out an old fellow who ground horseradish and put it into jars to sell at the Public Market. Sometimes I really did help him, and he'd give me a quarter if he was feeling good. He lived in a houseboat tied to an old pier on Lake Union, and I tell you that if the Health Department had ever thought to look into that houseboat, they would have hanged him!"

Beck's mother was the chief support of the family. She was his heroine all her 94 years and brought him up with no nonsense. He was a good boy, earnest, a hard worker. He never smoked, never played a game of pool, never drank. "I don't know why, I just didn't," Beck said. "I used to go off alone and read. I loved books."

If he had a fault, it was dodging the truant officer. Schools weren't so rigid in those days about absenteeism, not unless a boy was a troublemaker. "Although I liked school," Beck said, "what I could earn by skipping class was important to the family."

"I will never forget how hard my mother worked to keep the family together," Beck recalls. "She had a job in a laundry at 8th and Olive. There were no regular hours, except that she had to be at work at seven in the morning and she worked in the flatwork department—sheets, pillow-cases, table covers, etc. until the job was finished. My sister and I would go up to the laundry nights and wait outside until she was through. It was seven or eight o'clock before she was done, and there wasn't any overtime pay.

I'd heard something about unions, and believe me, it was then and there that I decided they were all to the good. I can still see myself and my little sister sitting on the curb outside that laundry while our mother drudged on into the night behind those sweaty windows. And off in the distance lived the rich and their ornate houses on Capitol Hill. I resolved to be as good as any of them. Ironically, the first full-time job I ever had (in 1914) was running a washroom wringer. *Like mother, like son.*

"Mom, Reta and I often ate out. After 12, 13 hours on her feet, mother was just too tired to rush home and prepare supper. So the three of us would go to this little Chinese cafe around the corner and order a big bowl of noodles with a little meat in them. We knew the cook, a Chinaman, and he would furnish us with three little empty bowls so we could divide them up. Total bill: 35 cents.

"I first started selling newspapers when we lived at 815 Pike Street and I was attending Cascade School. I was eight or nine years old then, about the time Harry Tracy, the bandit, was making news. Tracy is down in history as one of the more notorious criminals ever in the Pacific Northwest. He escaped from the penitentiary at Salem, Oregon, came to Bothell, near Seattle, and then fled to eastern Washington, where he murdered several people before killing himself in a wheat field in a shootout with police. The *Seattle Times* and the *Seattle Star* put out extras on the story and I cleaned up. As I remember, newspapers sold for 3 cents, half of which went to me. My profit was based on how many papers I could sell. You had to be a hustler to make it pay. Howard Parish, later the editor of the *Seattle Star*, sold papers with me in those days.

"From the age of 12 to the age of 14 or 15, I had a *P-I* route delivering papers in a district where the elite lived. I had about 350 customers, the biggest route in the *P-I's* chain, and I worked seven days a week. The route extended from Pine to Madison, and from Terry to Broadway. It was impossible to carry 350 papers at once, so I broke them up into two packs. The streetcar went up Pike Street and dropped off half my load at the corner of Boren Avenue for me; I picked up the second load at old Seattle High School, left there by the streetcar, and finished my route.

"I continued to carry papers through my first year of high school. As I grew, I carried both the *P-I* and the *Times*. That meant getting up at 5 a.m. for the *P-I* and working after school for the *Times*. Those were long days. I got $12 a month from the *Times* and $3.15 a week from the *P-I*.

"Sound like hard work? It was, but it was nothing compared to those times when I first broke in selling papers. I didn't have a standard route then, only street corners, and we had to fight for the good corners. We'd get our papers, station ourselves on a corner, and then hold it for as long as we could, until a bigger kid came along and muscled us out. If it was an especially good corner, you just put down your papers and fought the guy. The winner kept the corner. The fighting got so bad that Seattle judges were forced to step in and decide which of us got which corners. Those decisions were backed up by the newspapers too. In other words if you developed a corner, you were protected by the circulation departments.

"Afterward, when I got a route of my own, I walked at least seven miles per trip, traversing back and forth throughout the neighborhoods. Then I'd walk back down to Lake Union, where we lived at 1207 Aloha, and eat breakfast. After, I'd go down to the lakeshore and collect bark and store it for winter stove wood. *Then* I'd go to school, walking from the south end of Lake Union to Broadway High School. That was a lot of daily walking, but it developed a marvelous pair of legs and a stout physique that has stood me in good stead all these years.

"School sports? Some. I was too light for high school football, only 115 pounds. I worked out at the downtown Seattle Athletic Club with some of the leading amateur prizefighters, several of whom won Pacific Coast and U.S. championships. Of course, I was always a rabid baseball fan. I followed the old Pacific Coast League and the Northwest League. In fact, as a kid, I even served as a batboy for a time. I had to give it up when my newspaper route kept getting in the way.

"I don't want it to sound like my boyhood was all drudgery. There was time for some play. I was a pretty good ballplayer. When I was 17, I played some semipro baseball around Seattle. I was never good enough to qualify for organized ball, but I was a damned good amateur player. I started to play golf on weekends. Then I started getting interested in the labor movement, and I found out very quickly I had to choose between golf and attending to business. Golf lost. I've never played it since.

"During World War I, I joined the Navy and was sent to Killingholme, England, as a machinist's mate. I flew over the North Sea in lumbering Curtiss flying boats on anti-Zeppelin patrols. Unlike the infantry, there was nothing monotonous about the war in the air. It was full of surprises, for those were the pioneer days when no one knew very much about flying. They had no fear except the fear of the unknown. Royal Flying Corps instructors called their cadets 'Huns' because they destroyed more British planes than the German Air Force did. There was no school of acrobatics for cadets. If a student asked an instructor how to loop a slow-flying training plane, he was told to put the nose of his craft down for speed and then pull back on the stick when the wings began to flap. Presently, the top brass became chary of that informal method and passed out a mimeographed slip with instructions printed on it. The first half was headed 'How to Get Into Trouble in the Air,' and it told the cadets what to do with their controls in order to stunt. The second half was titled 'How to Get Out of Trouble in the Air.' One cadet tore off the first part, wadded it up, and threw it away. 'If you don't read that,' he grunted, 'you won't need this,' and he wadded up the second part and threw that away, too."

Beck says that we must always remember when we

think of World War I that everyone was endowed with the supreme courage of ignorance. The young men who flew the machines back then were carefree fellows with waxed mustaches (if they were old enough to grow one at all), polished boots, and an aloof carriage, which they cultivated assiduously to conceal the fact that their youth and curiosity had betrayed them into the paths of acute insanity. One of their biggest hazards was their own minds, their own imaginations. It helped if a flyer had a sense of humor.

Arch Whitehouse, author of numerous air adventure stories, was a fighter pilot in WWI, rising to the rank of flight commander. He was officially credited with 16 enemy aircraft. His career coincided almost to the month with that of Baron von Richthofen, the German ace, and he did battle with the German Flying Circus several times over that period of time. Whitehouse once told me the difference between the two world wars.

"The soldiers of World War II didn't even remotely resemble our breed of 1914-1918," he said. "World War I was grim, granted, and we got badly beaten sometimes, but we also managed to laugh. I saw this comparison in the Second World War, when I was a war correspondent. I flew a lot with our boys and was close to all the Allied flying services, and it seemed to me, this wasn't the war I knew. These weren't the fellows I flew with in the first war. The ghosts of all our old flying buddies kept laughing over my shoulder."

"Dorothy, my first wife, and I were married in June of 1918," Beck continued. "I was home on furlough after Navy boot training down at North Island, California. We got married in the morning, and that afternoon I left for San Diego to join a bombing squad being deployed on the North Sea for the length of the war. I didn't even have 24 hours with my new bride; then off to war for 14 months before seeing her again. What a honeymoon!

"Hundreds of thousands of gasoline and petrol tanks

were stored at our station. Our main job was supplying submarines, and our fighter planes were kept busy driving enemy Zeppelins back. Those Zeppelins would sneak in trying to destroy our fuel dumps, then go on to London in an attempt to shake up civilian morale. We knocked some of them out of the sky.

"Flying really got in my blood. I have flown roughly 5,000,000 miles in my lifetime. Long before I was elected president of the Teamsters, I had already logged a million miles. I was the first officer in the union allowed to fly. When Dan Tobin, then the president, first heard about it, he hit the roof. He ordered me to stop. I told him no. 'Either I go on flying or I quit.' He said, 'Well, go ahead and break your neck,' and I got my way.

"After the Armistice was declared in 1918, I returned to America on a troopship with 29,000 other servicemen. Among those aboard was baseball's great Ty Cobb. He wore the bars of a captain and had been serving in Chemical Warfare Service as an instructor with the Gas and Flame Division. George Sisler, Branch Rickey, and Christy Mathewson belonged to the same unit.

"Our ship tied up at Pelham Bay Park in New York in December. Immediately, all the guys in uniform started angling for early discharges. I was still under a four-year enlistment with the Navy, but I filed an application for release in the form of a letter. I explained that I was married and emphasized that my young bride of 14 months was very sick. (I honestly had no knowledge of any illness, I just made the story up.) The letter went right out to Seattle, where it was quickly turned over to the Red Cross for investigation. Within three days back came a letter recommending immediate discharge. I was amazed. I got my discharge and caught a train out of New York that evening. My entire bankroll totaled $1.80 in small change, all I had for 3,000 miles to Seattle. There was a brief stopover in Cleveland and I got out to buy donuts and coffee. Now I was down to $1.40. As I was counting my change, this guy came up to me, stuck a gun in my ribs, and took the money. That's the God's honest truth, too. When I got back on the train and told everybody about my bad luck, they passed a hat around and took up a collection. The result was I landed in Seattle with $1.20 *more* than when I left New York.

"Now for the clincher. My father and sister met me at the train depot and drove me home. Where was Dorothy? Well, she had been staying with my parents at 1302 Valley Street and, by God, was sick in bed. For four months, she hadn't been able to hear a thing. She was stone deaf, a victim of the great Seattle influenza epidemic of 1918. Thank heaven, she pulled through and her hearing returned. But just consider the coincidence: Dreaming up a phony story to get out of the Navy, thinking I was lying like hell, when in truth, she really *was* ill."

When Jack Connors, an old friend of the family and an avid union man, heard that Dave was home, he marched right over and sought his help. Dave, still in uniform, hadn't even unpacked yet, but that didn't stop Connors.

"Dave," he said, "the newspapers are talking about a general strike here. Shipyard workers are walking off the job. Everybody is calling for a general strike in sympathy with them."

Beck got a copy of the morning paper. On the front page, Mayor Ole Hanson had painted a grim picture.

"He sounds like a political blowhard to me," Dave snorted.

"No, it's the truth," Connors insisted. "The labor situation is very dim. Dave, you must do something."

"Me?" Beck said. "I'm just home from the war. Why me?"

"Because the fellows respect you," Connors said. "They'll listen to you. We're holding an emergency meeting of our laundry union this very night. Come on down to the hall and speak to them."

Beck had put on considerable weight. The only suit

that fit him was the sailor uniform he had on.

"Don't worry," Connors said. "Actually, the sailor suit might even help."

So Mother Beck brushed up her son's blues and pressed them while Connors and Dave outlined his speech in the bedroom. Connors was terribly upset, and the thought of a general strike bothered Dave, too.

"Before the war I had had a brief experience with a strike and hated it," Dave said. "I still hate strikes. Sure, the Teamsters had plenty of them under Dan Tobin, and later when I was on the way to the presidency, but I have always regarded a strike as a last resort. I believe I was the first union leader to take that position. Any crackpot can work up a strike vote, but it takes sensible effort (on both sides) to avoid one. I always demanded the right to strike.

"So, the idea of a general strike in Seattle curdled my blood. Connors was no alarmist, I knew that. Some of the Teamster unions already had voted to hit the bricks and that concerned me more. The idea of a general strike was only a theory in America. It was something that happened in Europe occasionally and always raised the roof in the process. Connors explained that the shipyard workers were demanding $8 a day for skilled labor, $5.50 for unskilled, with a 44-hour work week. I told him they must have gone crazy.

"I don't remember what I said that night. The meeting was not covered by the press, so there is no record of it. But whatever I told them must have convinced the membership that a general strike was a revolution, actually anarchy. I really stood them on their feet, and how good that felt to a fuzz-chinned kid in a sailor suit.

"When we went into the meeting, 110 unions already had voted for 'anarchy'; when we came out, the Laundry and Dye Works Drivers Local 566 had said 'no.' We were the only Teamster union to vote that way.

"The general strike made a deep impression on me. I was a union member and always will be. Unions are a part of the national economy, although even now there are still a few diehards trying to break them up. I believed in World War I—and the second World War, too—and I figured we had fought for democracy. But back there in 1919 I came home, and before I could get back into a laundry truck, I ran into something that was the direct opposite of democracy. *Right in my own country and my own home-town.* That Anna Louise Strong they made such a fuss about was fuzzy in the head; she was an old-time suffra-gette in the wrong pew when it came to labor. It was then and there, during the general strike, that I had it proved to me that communism had nothing for labor. If ever they got the chance they would crucify labor right off the bat. Look what happened in Russia.

"My opposition to the general strike was not entirely due to my hatred of the Reds. Our local had a contract and so did the other Teamster unions. I was preaching the sanctity of contracts when a whole hell of a lot of union leaders were still preaching what amounted to class warfare.

"After the war, I went back to Seattle and asked for my old job back at Central Laundry. The place had been sold and my old boss, a Mr. Ragsdale, had taken over my route. As a returning serviceman, I was entitled to my old job, but Mr. Ragsdale was 70 years old and a good friend of my parents and I didn't want him to lose his job. 'No,' I told the new manager, 'let Mr. Ragsdale keep the route. I can get another job a lot easier than he can.' So I went to work for Mutual Laundry, owned and operated by the un-ion. I was assigned a route out in the University District. I drove an old Ford truck, one of those traps with the old planetary gear system. As my route expanded, I moved up to an engine with a chain drive. If it'd ever broken down, I would have been in a jam. I wasn't worth a damn as a mechanic—wouldn't have been worth $2 a year to any-body. Oh, I could tinker with a motor, if somebody stood over my shoulder and told me what to do, but when it in-volved such intricacies as transmission and differential and crankshaft, I was lost. I was a lousy mechanic, then as well as now.

"I'd start out in the morning at 5:30, swing around Queen Anne Hill, stopping along the way to pick up loads of clothes, and then hurry back to the laundry to be in the wet wash at 7:30. Wet-washing is completely gone now, because of the development of washing machines. It was hard work, but I made good money, more than $100 a week. I was on that job for about two years before I was made route manager. Then I had an argument with the supervisor over working conditions; he refused to change, and I walked off the job. Back at Central Laundry, Mr. Ragsdale was retiring and I got my old route back. I stayed there until 1924.

"I decided to run for secretary of the local union, a position held by Fred Wyatt from the day of its inception. In my campaign against him I pointed out in my speeches that the drivers were being shortchanged; that wages, hours, and conditions were below par. I won the election rather easily and started as secretary-treasurer on December 1, 1924.

"The following year the convention of the International Brotherhood of Teamsters was scheduled to meet in Seattle. As secretary-treasurer of the Laundry Drivers Union, I joined the Joint Council and was elected secretary of that. Subsequently, I was named chairman of the Arrangements Committee for the Teamster Convention.

"The first time in my life I ever saw Dan Tobin was when he walked off the boat coming down from Vancouver, British Columbia. He had traveled west via Canada on the Canadian Pacific, then took a boat to Seattle, where Mike Casey of San Francisco, who was my superior officer on the coast, and I met him at the dock. That was the first time I ever laid eyes on Daniel J. Tobin.

"When the Railroad Brotherhood came into Seattle and invested large sums of money merging 15 laundries down to six, I was still secretary-treasurer of the Laundry Drivers Union. Those behind the merger offered me $200 a week if I'd quit the labor movement and go with them. I tele-

Lemuel and Mary Beck, Dave's parents. His father died in 1920. His mother died at 94 while Dave was in McNeil Island Penitentiary. This photo was taken at Alki Beach approximately 1915.

Dave and Reta Beck at ages 14 and 12.

Dave Beck at approximately age 30 when he was Exalted Ruler, Seattle Lodge No. 92 of the Elks.

Dave Beck Jr. and his father at Dave Beck Jr.'s graduation from Officer Candidate's School. Dave Beck Jr. served as a commissioned officer of the U.S. Army Transport Division in the South Pacific during World War II.

Old Seattle High football team in 1911. Arrow at upper right identifies Dave Beck.

Navy "boot camp" in 1917 with Dave Beck in lower row second from right.

Dave Beck as Grand Exalted Ruler of Elks is congratulated by Robert Macfarlane.

(Below) Dave Beck with Seattle Mayor John F. Dore in 1937.

Dave Beck began his long history as a Teamster as the driver of a Model T laundry truck in Seattle.

During 1951 Beck toured Pacific rim to inspect U.S. defense bases.

The late William Green, A.F. of L. President, with Dave Beck.

phoned Mike Casey, who'd been something of a mentor to me, and told him I was seriously considering the offer. Mike said he knew Dan Tobin wouldn't want me to leave. I wasn't yet on the Teamster payroll, and I told Casey I had to make a living. Lewis Schwellenbach and Robert Mac-farlane—the first would eventually become Secretary of Labor, the other president of the Northern Pacific Railway—were law partners in Seattle, with some big laundries among their clients. They were the ones putting the laundry merger together. I was flattered and greatly tempted by their offer to hire me as route manager of the new combine. I had become a father.

"I told Casey, 'I want money and need security, but I want to stay with the union.'

"'Well,' Casey said, 'hold off for a few days before giving 'em your answer. I'll talk to Tobin.'

"Casey took my dilemma to the Teamster boss, and Tobin offered me a job as part-time general organizer for the International. It paid $500 a month and $5 a day for miscellaneous expenses. Tobin said I could keep my job with the laundry drivers until I had broken in a replacement, and then he'd raise my salary another $100. I accepted, and in time I became a full-time organizer in charge of the whole Pacific Northwest and British Columbia.

"That's how I got involved with the Teamsters. I don't know what I would have done with my life if I hadn't accepted Tobin's offer; probably would have wound up in the laundry business. In high school I entertained the prospect of going to law school. I had my heart and mind set on becoming a lawyer. That's the one regret I still have. But there was no way I could have afforded law school. What money I earned was siphoned off to help my parents make ends meet. My father was a wonderful man and a big influence on me, but he was absolutely the world's worst businessman. Later, after I got married, my father-in-law, superintendent of the Dexter-Horton Building, talked about me to an attorney who had an office there. The lawyer's name was Lewis, and he invited me to come down and read law with him. I did that in my spare time for three or four years, and Mr. Lewis urged me to go on to law school. I couldn't spare another four years, however. By then I was making such giant strides with the Teamsters that I dropped all future consideration of law. When you think about all the courtroom appearances I have made over the years, though, that law training would have come in handy.

6

Growing
Pains

A very vital person in the life of Dave Beck
was Ann Watkins (now Kotin), his personal secretary for
31 years. She first came into his life in 1927.

Ann had been employed as secretary to the manager of
the Superior Service Laundry in Seattle, with offices at
11th and East Spring. Because of his union connections,
Dave often visited the office. One June morning of '27 he
walked in and caught Ann frowning. That was unusual,
because she had a sunny disposition to go with her tall,
winsome good looks. Everybody loved Ann Watkins, even
Old Scrooge down the block.

Dave sidled up to her desk and said, "What's the
matter with you today? Where's that big smile?"

Ann sighed.

"I'm just disgusted," she told him. "They've been
promising me a raise here for months. I just got my check
and it's still $22.50."

Without preliminaries, Dave asked, "Well, how would
you like to go to work for me? I will give you $27.50 a week,

with two weeks vacation." He also mentioned the hours and conditions. Just then Madge Claudon, the office manager, came out of her office. Dave was the first to speak.

"Madge," he said, "I have just offered Ann a job."

He named the salary, $27.50, which was what Madge was getting. Madge said nothing, showed no emotion whatsoever, and the subject was dropped. A few moments later, Dave left.

That afternoon, Ann received a phone call from Dave. He told her, "Madge must have talked to your boss. He's objecting to the offer I made you. He says I'm taking his confidential girl away from Superior. If he and the others down there knew as much about their business as I do, they wouldn't be in the shape they're in. For now, there isn't much I can do about bringing you over here with me."

Ann Watkins Kotin told me—

"In those days, we worked Saturdays. I put in a lot of hours for $22.50 a week. So on the morning of October 1, 1927, I opened my pay envelope and it was the same amount—no raise. I murmured to myself, 'Well, that does it! I'm quitting!' Mr. Barnhart, the secretary-treasurer, had his office next to mine. I went in and said, 'Mr. Barnhart, I'm leaving. In view of the differences we've had, I don't think I owe you any notice. My mind is made up.'

"Mr. Barnhart looked straight at me and said, 'Are you going to work for Dave Beck?'

"'I haven't thought about it, but I'll phone him,' I said. 'That's a good idea.'

"I telephoned Dave, on this Saturday before noon, and he happened to pick up the receiver. I explained that I had just quit my job and was his offer still good? He told me to report to work on Monday morning. That was the 3rd of October, 1927, and I was with him to the last Friday, 1958.

"On the first day I went to work for him, he gave me some fatherly advice. He put his hand on my shoulder, and said, 'Ann, I want to talk to you about something. You're young, you are attractive, and you are going to be working around men who are going to ask you for dates. If I were you, I would keep my social life completely separate from my business life. Don't take a drink during the day, because you might come back to the office and have differences with someone who comes in to pay his union dues and he will smell your breath and say you were drunk.'

"He gave me some very sound advice which stood me in good stead for all the years, and he was Mr. Beck to me till the day he left the presidency."

In the late Twenties, the mood between workers and employers continued to fester. Seattle's general strike of 1919 had left feelings raw and sensitive. The Wobblies had gone into lumber camps and sawmills with their radical preaching and militant tactics and sparked off bloody, bone-cracking clashes with thugs hired by the employers. Like faithful domestic animals, the plug-uglies were eager to perform any task ordered by their masters. It was one of the strangest arrays of palookas ever assembled in the Pacific Northwest; cauliflower ears, squashed noses, and beef on the hoof that moved with the lumbering grace of a bull moose answering the call of the lovelorn.

In this atmosphere of political militancy, Dave Beck was an anomaly. He wrote off the Wobblies as a bunch of crackpots. "I have no strong political feelings either way," he commented at the time. "I believe in the free enterprise system. All I want for our members is a fair share of the profits; no more, no less."

Beck made it clear that the best way to go about this was to organize everyone and everything in sight and so be able to bargain collectively with the employers.

He told his members, "The employers are not bad men. But, quite naturally, they're not going to give us any more than they have to. They are crazy if they do. We'll have to bargain and fight for everything we get."

If Beck had anything against the free enterprise system, it was its untidiness. "Through competition," he said in 1927, "the price structure is inconsistent. That, in turn, forces the wage structure to be unpredictable—and that tends to hurt the Teamsters."

So in 1927 Beck got the Laundry Association to sign a contract with the laundry drivers' local calling for the drivers' commissions to be based on a uniform price list. "The laundries are free to charge whatever they want to for their service," Beck said. "They can even give it away if they choose, but the drivers will be paid a standard fee. Wages are 42 percent of the total cost of a laundry's operation. This new contract will go a long way toward establishing a fair competitive structure." Thus the laundry business was finally stabilized. "To some people," Beck explained, "the arrangement looked like price fixing, but the courts decided it was not." After that, Beck went on to "stabilize" many other industries.

During the first decade of his organizing adventures, employers and the general public were mystified by Beck and his associates. They didn't know whether to trust him or not. But he plunged ever onward. He next managed to organize the "over-the-road" drivers, the truck jockeys who whipped the big machines up and down the Pacific Coast, into what became known as the Highway Drivers Council. Uneasy employers guessed correctly that he was preparing a big stick to get them into line or face the prospect of seeing their freight deliveries shut off.

As Beck's rough-and-tumble "beef squads" picked up steam, the 1930s were marked by public turmoil and controversy over incidents of head-cracking and window-smashing. There was ugly antagonism toward Beck on the part of many business and civic organizations in the state. That feeling extended from Seattle to the agricultural areas of eastern Washington when unionists tangled with farmers driving trucks to market. "Beef squads" became a common newspaper expression; an unsolved accident on the property of an "unfair" employer here, a cut-rate dry cleaning shop blown up there; trucks upset and rammed by cars equipped with steel-rail bumpers.

Philosophically, Beck went by his own rule book.

"I am a great believer in fighting an adversary under any type of rule book he elects to use," Beck said. "I believe in fair play, but only if our opponents do likewise. If they get out in the gutter, I'll get out in the gutter with them. But they'll make the first move to be there, not me.

"Newspapers frequently accused us of carrying ball bats into our jurisdictional disputes. No, we never used ball bats. Sure, my men were a tough lot, but they didn't pack clubs. I remember the 1934 jurisdictional fights we had with the breweries. They were financed by the Brewery Workers International Union. They didn't use ball bats against us, either. What they did use was much more useful: *guns*! That was a fight to the finish. Ann, my secretary, remembers the details. She can tell you how the blood flowed—and a lot of it was *our* blood."

"We were deep in this bloody jurisdictional battle with the Brewery Workers International Union and our people were picketing the Marinoff Brewery over in Tacoma," Ann Watkins Kotin recalls. "One of our pickets was Tom Leo, a great big buster of a guy. We nicknamed him Slim. He stood 6'-3" and had shoulders as broad as a 10-ton truck. Slim worked the picket line night and day. Nights, he slept on the ground, wearing only a little skimpy shirt to keep him warm. I drove over to Tacoma several times to check on our fellows and could see the shadows of people in the upper windows of the brewery with guns. Slim Leo and some of the other guys were standing in a field, across from the brewery, keeping a watch on the situation when Frank Brewster showed up. He took one look at Slim shivering in the cold and went right down and bought him a sheepskin-lined jacket. 'Here,' he told Slim, 'put this on—and while you're at it, for God's sake, go to the barbershop and get a shave.' And Slim Leo said, 'Aw, to hell with it; let the *coroner* shave me.' That was what Slim thought of his chances of coming out of that brewery fight alive.

"One of our people did die. His name was Usitalo—shot right through the forehead in an automobile chase. I don't know who killed him. Dave says it was Pete Marinoff; I don't know. I do know that Usitalo wasn't carrying any weapons when he was shot; no gun, no knife, not even a club."

"Our fight with the brewery workers union is very simple to explain," Beck interrupted. "Under the constitution of the A.F. of L., they had jurisdiction for *inside* brewery workers, and we had it over drivers and helpers. That was the basis of the argument right there. Pure and simple, they violated our jurisdiction. The A.F. of L. supported our position time after time, yet the BWIU cockily tried to force us to accept its position, even though the right of law was on our side. So it came down to bloodshed. The only way to settle it was in an open fight.

"Johnny O'Leary, a fine prizefighter, was another Teamster who was killed—not in the brewery fight, but in our scuffles with the taxicabs. The manager of the Yellow Cab Company in Seattle killed him. Strange, isn't it, that the public blamed us for dirty tactics, yet in all the blood lust, only two people lost their lives—and both were Teamsters. They carried no guns or knives.

"I remember once when trouble was on the verge of exploding at a warehouse down at Eighth Avenue Southwest. I received a telephone call from Captain Hedges of the police department. He said, 'Dave, I need a favor.' I asked him, 'What is it?' He said, 'For crying out loud, get down here and stop these guys from fighting.' I asked him, 'What are you talking about, Captain? They're not fighting; they are all down there by themselves.' And he said, 'Hell, when they haven't anybody else to fight, they fight *each other*.' Oh, those were crazy times."

In the fall of 1936, more than 500 women, bearing signs

reading DOWN WITH BECK-ISM, stormed the state capitol at Olympia. They insisted that the governor take immediate action to protect farmers and other citizens from strikes and war-like abuses which they blamed on Beck and his beef squads. Beck piously denied the charges. "The work of some hothead," he told reporters. "But you must remember that employers are fighting us with every dirty trick in the book. Naturally, if they want to fight that way, labor has to fight fire with fire."

Beck stoutly rejected the claim that he personally advocated or countenanced violence. "Industry has brought it on," he shouted. "They are trying to control labor by force."

But Dave Beck was far more than a mere deployer of muscle. Perhaps more than anyone else, he understood the immense power of the Teamsters in an industrial nation that transported its vital supplies on the wheels of some 10 million trucks. By refusing to deliver those supplies, the Teamsters could strangle business; by refusing to support other unions, the Teamsters could break strikes. Beck took the fullest advantage of his power. A genuine organizational genius, he looked south from his Seattle stronghold and saw how he could force his Teamsters on unorganized Los Angeles by threatening to cut off its supplies from the north. The answer lay in regional organization.

"For a long time I studied how to organize southern California and especially Los Angeles," Beck recalls. "Traditionally, L.A. was an 'open shop' town. But it was out of my jurisdiction. In 1937 Dan Tobin made me chief organizer for the West Coast. I promptly moved into action with an invention of my own: The Western Conference of Teamsters." It has been called "the most brilliant organizing device ever created."

Beck continued, "Up till then, the individual locals of the union had almost total independence. There was only haphazard cooperation among them and very little interchange of ideas or information. In the old days this lack of interstate communication was accepted, because communities were pretty self-contained. But as America grew, I saw that union organization would have to adapt itself to the changing pattern of the economy. The C.I.O.'s 'vertical unionism' was one answer; that is, erasing craft lines to include all workers in a factory and all factories in an industry. My solution was to throw the Teamsters' entire 11-state area into one big, centrally-controlled organizing structure. What's more, in what we called 'protecting the flanks,' we'd organize not only everything on wheels but peripheral and supporting fields such as warehousemen, parking lot attendants, and so forth.

"Well, by encircling and blockading Los Angeles, we took the metropolis like General Grant took Richmond. Truck drivers in L.A. could join the union or not. But—if trucking companies tried to deliver goods to other cities, the Teamsters and our affiliates in these places could not be expected to handle this 'hot cargo' at the other end. Nor could Los Angeles merchants expect to receive goods from outside except by union drivers, who, of course, could not be expected to deliver to nonunion businesses. That was that. When we first went into L.A. we had less than 400 members; when we finished organizing, we had over 100,000.

"I used the same technique (fortified by the 'beef squads') to break the back of the brewery workers' union in the Pacific Northwest. The jurisdictional quarrel had been an old one, and the rights and wrongs of the matter are too tangled and controversial to go into here. In any case, the result was that I vowed that the brewery workers, *inside* workers as well as truck drivers, had to belong to the Teamsters. To drive home my point, I embargoed all beer except that made by breweries which signed up with our union. The fight lasted for many months; inevitably, we won in the end. All West Coast beer is made today under the auspices of the Teamsters.

"Other strange companions soon found themselves joining forces with us: cannery workers, aircraft warehousemen, automobile salesmen, office employes, rag sorters—even optical technicians. Although without the political motive of the I.W.W., I seemed to be heading in the direction of one big union. At the same time I felt competent to judge the merits of the case when other unions put on organizing strikes. Often I disapproved. On my orders Teamsters went through picket lines many times when they violated our jurisdiction.

"The way we were now organized—the way we were growing by leaps and bounds—we could launch a fight in every nook and corner of the 11 western states. I and my associates had fought and struggled and worked like hell to bring the Teamsters to that position.

"People no longer called me 'Public Goon No. 1.' Now they called me something nearer 'Public Benefactor No. 1.' In this I was greatly aided by Harry Bridges, alleged pro-communist head of the West Coast longshoremen. Bridges swung his union into the newly formed C.I.O. and in 1937 began his 'inland march' designed to add warehousemen and eventually, presumably, other categories of workers to his domain. I was not cognizant of his intentions, but I knew goddamn well what he was up to. It was a direct challenge to me and the Teamsters. The result was a limited but bloody civil war. The longshoremen's favorite weapon was the cargo hook; we favored bare knuckles. We won the war, and in the process earned the gratitude of inland employers who feared him much more than they did us.

"After that, one employer and trade association after another tumbled into our arms. The C.I.O. had designs on the retail clerks. Immediately the clerks found themselves urged by their employers to join a new union organized by me with headquarters housed in our building. Bridges had made a speech at the University of Washington predicting the end of the employer class. In my next speech I attacked his philosophy:

"'I do not subscribe in the slightest degree to Harry Bridges' claim that there is no place in the economic and social life of our country for employers. Yes, we work with industry. We positively admit it. But no man alive can say he paid Dave Beck 5 cents for the conduct or regulation of his business. No man can say there is a single communist in our union. If any communist sticks his head up, we'll throw him out.'"

For Dave Beck, the Teamster wagon was the perfect vehicle for a ride to the top. At its first convention in 1903, with Niagara Falls roaring in the background, the 50,000-member International Brotherhood of Teamsters selected as its first president a 295-pound cutthroat named Cornelius Shea, who eventually was packed off to Sing Sing for stabbing his mistress 27 times (he bungled the job—the girl lived). Next in 1907 came Irish-born Tobin, who was to hold office for 45 astonishing years. Fond of boasting that he ran the union with only two staffers, Tobin came to rule over an empire that had 1,000,000 members, only after Beck's organizational policy was adopted. The Teamsters claimed a net worth of $25 million and had enormous economic and political power. In 1944, when President Franklin Roosevelt made his famed fourth-term campaign speech at a Teamsters' dinner on how mad his dog, Fala, was getting at Roosevelt critics, Tobin sat at his side.

Beck remembers those days:

While Tobin was not a good organizer (he couldn't have organized his mother), he was the slickest politician I have ever known in the labor movement. I had the highest regard for him. Yet I don't suppose anyone in his entire career had more disagreements with him. One time he summoned me to Denver for a meeting of the General Executive Board. He wanted me to disband the Western Conference of Teamsters. Now, I hadn't had permission to form it in the first place; I just went ahead and set it up. Catching on as rapidly as it did and functioning so fluidly, I thought Tobin and the Board would be pleased. They weren't.

"Go back to Seattle and dissolve it," Tobin told me.

"I'll do no such thing," I said. "I will give you my resignation first."

Tobin did not get mad. He just looked at me.

"Listen, Dan," I said. "Be reasonable. Why don't you let our Western Conference go for four months? You're coming out to San Francisco then for a conference; why not wait till then to make a decision? Look it over first, and if you are still intent on closing us down, I'll give you my resignation and no hard feelings."

Tobin agreed to wait.

The conference opened on a Monday, I called on Tobin for a few words. He rose and said he was there primarily to observe the Western Conference of Teamsters. He said he would wait until Friday, when the conference ended, before announcing his decision. On Friday he got up, and this time he was smiling.

"I've been in the Trade Union Movement since 1901," he told the delegates. "I've never seen anything even close to what you have organized out here. Personally, I'm for it."

With Tobin's support, we were written into the constitution of Teamsters International and after that played a big role in making the union the largest in the world.

Thinking of Dan Tobin, I remember we were attending a meeting of the Executive Council of the A.F. of L. in Miami Beach, Florida. While there, we were invited to be the guests of the Cuban government over in Havana. It turned out to be a very fancy affair; a beautiful banquet, dancing, gambling in the adjoining casino, and *formal* dress. None of us had brought along dinner clothes. No one had warned us about it being formal. An exception was made in our case, and we were given a very choice table right next to the dance floor. Drinks were served, and soon Tobin was feeling no pain. Now, when Dan got to drinking, and drinking too much, more food went down the front of his vest than into his mouth. As the evening progressed, we grew very aware of all the beautifully gowned women around us—from Cuba, from the British West Indies, from the United States—and the glances they were tossing at us. Finally, this gorgeously gowned beauty came over. I was sitting next to Mike Casey, Tobin was across from us, and she looked straight at us and, noting our street clothes, said, "PIGS!" I'd have given $10,000, if I'd had it, for the floor to open up and swallow us up.

After dinner we went into the casino. Gambling was in full swing. The crap tables, roulette wheel, blackjack, and slot machines were crowded. Now, Tobin, in my opinion, was one of the worst gamblers I ever knew. He started out at the crap table, moved to roulette, blackjack, and then the slots. Nothing is coming up right for him. Pretty soon he comes back to Casey and says, "Mike, gimme $500." In all the years I knew him, he never borrowed a dollar from me. Whether he considered me too young (he had sons older than I was), I don't know. But he asked Mike, and Mike said, "Yes, Mr. President." Mike reached into his pants pocket and pulled out five $100 bills. Tobin took it and returned to a crap table. Fifteen minutes later he was back. "Mike, let me have another $500." Mike fished out $500 more. Twenty minutes later, Tobin wants another $500. Mike gave it to him. Within 10 minutes, Tobin asks for another $500. "Mr. President," Mike said, "I'm down to my last $300." "Well," Tobin said, "let me have it." Tobin went back to the tables and 15 minutes afterward he was back asking for another $500.

Mike Casey was plainly exasperated by this time. "Mr. President," he said to Tobin, "I told you the last time you were here that I only had $300 left—and I gave that to you."

"Mike," Tobin said, "you don't have a very good memory. In all the years we've been traveling together you've told me 50 times that you never left home without following the old Irish custom of sewing $500 in your underwear."

Tobin pointed to the gent's room.

"Now, get over there and unsew that money."

Mike Casey went to the men's room, stripped to his underwear and came back with the $500. Handing it to Tobin, Mike said, "I've heard of gamblers losing their shirts—but this is the first time I heard of anyone losing his shorts."

Thirty minutes later, Tobin was broke again, and we all went home.

One time my wife, Dorothy, joined the Tobins, Dan and Irene, at dinner at Miami Beach. Afterwards, Dan suggested the three of them drive to this gambling emporium outside town. I was not with them. I was out in Hollywood settling a labor dispute in the motion picture industry.

This night Dan's luck was much better. The dice were hot and he didn't want to quit. Irene came over to the crap table, reminded him it was 1 a.m., and said it was time to leave. Dan pushed her away. She pleaded with him to stop. Dan kept rolling the dice.

For some inexplicable reason, Dorothy had tremendous influence with Dan. Anything she wanted, he made sure she had. So Irene, sobbing by now, asked Dorothy to use her persuasion on Dan. Dorothy walked over to him and pulled on his elbow. "Dan," she said calmly, "I'm not feeling very well. May we go home? I'm tired."

"Right away," Dan said. He scooped up his winnings, cashed in his chips, and the three of them went out to the car. Dan had been drinking, so Dorothy drove. It was an 18-mile trip to the Tobins' home. Dorothy let Dan and Irene out in front of the house, then put the car in the garage. As she was slipping out of the front seat, her eyes fell on a package on the floor. Inside was a bundle of crisp, green bills—$5, $10, $20, $50 bills. She counted it. Nearly $1,800. Dorothy stuffed it into her handbag and went into the house.

Next morning, Dan and Dorothy shared breakfast. Irene slept in late. Dan remarked what a good time they had the evening before. Dorothy nodded. "Yes," she said. "And what a lucky night it was for you. You won a lot of money."

"I never won a dollar," Dan said.

"Yes, you did."

"Where?"

"I have it upstairs in my bag—$1,780. It was on the floor of the back seat of the car."

"Well, I'm not taking it; it's not my money."

"All right," Dorothy told him, "if you won't take it, I'll give it to Irene."

"No! No!" Dan protested. "I'll take it, if you say so. But, *please*—don't tell Irene I won it."

That was Dan Tobin. He played hard; he worked hard. He was a great character.

McCallum:

Dan Tobin and Dave Beck got along uncommonly well together. They were an ideal team. Tobin preferred life behind an old roll-back desk that must have been the world's worst in Indianapolis; Beck was more at home among the rank and file out in the field. One of the few times Tobin displayed a fit of temper toward Dave was in 1949, when Dave appeared on the cover of *Time* magazine. It had no sooner hit the newsstands than Dave got a telephone call from the president.

"Why in hell are *you* on the cover of *Time*?" shouted Tobin.

"How the hell do I know?" Beck yelled back. "Call *Time* and ask them."

Tobin was burned up because Beck was on the cover and he wasn't.

Afterward, the rush was on. Rumors flew like buckshot. Members of the press corps filled their articles and columns with conjecture: Dave Beck was going to be the next president of the Teamster International. Beck did his level best to cool the stories. "I will never be president of the Teamsters until Dan Tobin, in a constitutional convention, stands up and nominates me for election," Beck kept repeating to reporters. But the articles persisted. "The handwriting is on the wall," wrote the correspondent for the *New York Mirror*. "Beck has already been picked as Tobin's successor."

"All those published rumors embarrassed Dave," Ann Watkins Kotin told me. "To reassure Dan Tobin that he was not behind them, he called me in and dictated a long letter to him. He urged Tobin not to retire. He told him, 'You run and maintain the position of president of the International Union, and we will continue to do your work for you out in the field.' Dave was doing that too, heading up just about everything."

By now, Dave had gained the reputation as the labor movement's all-time supersalesman. Said another labor leader: "Dave Beck will take anybody he can get his hands on. A Teamster to him is anybody who sleeps on a bed with movable casters."

In the summer of 1952, Tobin asked Dave to visit him at his vacation place near Boston. He announced that he wanted to place Dave's name in nomination for the presidency. It was time that he stepped down, he said.

"Though you could not tell by his appearance—he still swam everyday, he took long walks—I think Dan Tobin sensed he was dying," Beck recalls. "I am certain his doctors had warned him to slow down. 'Dan,' I am sure he was advised, 'you've only got a while longer to live. It would be best if you retired and took care of yourself. Prolong your life for as long as possible.' Tobin never confided in me about his health, but as I look back on it now, I'm sure he knew his days were numbered."

October, 1952, finally came and, sure enough, Tobin got up in convention and nominated Dave with a soaring declaration: "There is not the slightest stain on his character. His conscience, I am confident, shines brilliantly in the eyes of God."

When the meeting broke up, news photographers asked

Tobin and Dave to pose for pictures together. Tobin looked pretty downhearted. After all, a long era was nearing the end for him. He had reigned for decades; now it was almost over. "Come on, *smile*," a photographer called out to him. And, Dan said, "How can I smile when I'm crying?"

"Frankly, if Tobin had chosen to run again, he could have defeated me," Beck said. "I mean that, too. Of course, a Tobin vs. Beck runoff was an impossibility, because I would have refused to allow myself to be nominated. That would have been like opposing my own father."

Actually, Dan Tobin lived on for three more years. He died in the fall of 1955. He lived just long enough to see the new $5½-million Teamster headquarters go up and his new offices as president emeritus.

"We visited Tobin for the last time in Indianapolis as he was dying," Ann Kotin said. "Dave, Einar Mohn, Al Woll, Tobin's son, Fred, and I all were at his bedside. Dan was just barely conscious, and Dave walked over to him and said, 'Dan, we have come to visit you. Fred is here. Einar is here, Al Woll is here.' He did not stir. Finally, 'Einar is here, Al Woll is here.' He still did not stir. Finally, softly, Dave told him, 'And Ann is here, too.' For the first time, there was movement. Tobin reached out weakly for my hand, and said, 'My Ann, my Ann,' and I reached across and clasped his hand in mine. His eyes focused on my face then, and he said, 'Ann, I'm dying.' I told him, 'Oh, no, come on now, you're not dying.' And he said, 'Oh, yes, Ann. We all must die—but we will meet again.'"

"I walked over to his side again," Beck recalls. "His voice was so faint that I had to put my ear down to his mouth to hear him. The last words he ever said to me were, 'Dave, I love you as I do my own sons.'"

As Dave Beck finished relating his part in the drama, I thought I saw a trace of tears in his eyes. He fell silent, for he did not trust himself to speak.

7

What a World!

THE POST World War I years were to become a spiraling, dizzy, mad, whirling planet of play; a wonderful, chaotic universe of clashing temperaments and human emotions unlike the world had ever witnessed before. Dynasties were to fall, nations collapse, politics change, dictators thunder, and geography torn apart by revolution. Distant wars were to come, yet here at home the trend was toward fun, fanfare, and frolic. What a world! What a country! What people!

Show business boomed. Charlie Chaplin starred in "The Kid," Al Jolson brought talkies to the movies in "The Jazz Singer," and ladies swooned at the sight of Rudolph Valentino. The dance marathon dazzled the nation, radio became a fact, and Charleston contests packed the dance halls.

The auto came of age. Now painted traffic lanes began to appear on streets and highways. It was every pedestrian for himself, now, as growing car accidents inspired the invention of safety bumpers.

General Billy Mitchell, who was the first to destroy a battleship from the air, was court-martialed for insubordination. Air-mail flights began from New York to San Francisco. Admiral Richard E. Byrd navigated history's first flight over the North Pole. And a lanky, thin-faced young aviator named Lindbergh thrilled the world as he flew his monoplane from New York to Paris nonstop.

There was news being made in the labor movement, too.

"By now, I had enrolled for extension courses at the University of Washington, eventually finishing law, commercial law, economics, business administration, history, and English," Beck told me. "I read a lot of books, mostly the autobiographies of successful men. I became something of a public speaker, a rhetorician. I can't remember the time when I wasn't making a speech. I turned into a William Jennings Bryan of the labor movement. I used to hammer away on just one subject: 'Organize.' By 1923 I had been elected president of the Teamsters Joint Council, an association of all the locals in the state. The next year I was elected secretary-treasurer of my own local. The following year, when the Teamsters held their international convention in Seattle, I was put in charge of the arrangements.

"The Roaring Twenties were very important to labor, because there was great organizing procedure going on all around. The war had ended and there were hundreds of thousands of men returning to civilian life. Due to the war there'd been a fantastic growth in industrial expansion, and there was a huge revamping in America's financial and business structure. Now there was growing agitation for unionization of personnel. Because of the shutdowns of war plants everywhere, unemployment was rampant. Right here in Seattle, the shipyards closed down practically overnight. That's what caused the city's general strike, the first such strike in the history of the U.S.A. It was a mess, I'll tell you."

After Dan Tobin made Beck an organizer in the Seattle area, Dave organized his men like an army. The year was 1926, and he blandly announced that several thousand of his members were taking jujitsu lessons "for their health." Beck says you have to understand the Seattle of the mid-1920s. The city then was still so new that many a citizen could remember shooting deer inside its limits. It was the product of great booms—the migration, which followed the railroad, the Alaskan gold stampede, the frenzied era of shipbuilding during the First World War. So when Beck went to work for the Teamsters, the gusty breath of all this excitement still hung in the air. The handsaws of lumber mills screamed along almost every lake and waterway. Loggers, fishermen, sailors, and bums lounged by the hundreds beside skid road missions, hash joints, and flophouses. Seattle's tough cops still took pride in using force sufficient to make an arrest and dragged in many a prisoner by the heels.

But for all this, and for all the eccentricities of Washington State politics, Seattle was a conservative city. It was crazy for education, community clubs, home cooking, Sunday automobile trips to Snoqualmie Falls and Mt. Rainier, and solid construction in municipal buildings. The core of its population was composed of thrifty, churchgoing Scandinavians who enjoyed the rain and yearned to own their own homes. It was a city which liked rose bushes. Dave Beck mirrored its conflicting personality. For years, however, Seattle was indignant at its own reflection.

In those days, becoming a labor organizer meant going to war. The history of labor in the Pacific Northwest was noisy with the crack of rifle fire, the crash of explosives, and the surrealistic thud of club on skull. The wildest battles had been set off by the I.W.W. (Wobblies) in its invasions of the woods and sawmills. In the celebrated Centralia, Washington massacre of 1919, Wobblies shot down four parading American Legionnaires; three years earlier in an equally bloody fight at Everett, Washington gun-toting deputy sheriffs killed or wounded 36 men with I.W.W. cards.

"The Wobblies were crazy," Beck said, stabbing at the air. "They were just a bunch of dynamite-loving, song-singing romantics who bayed for the class struggle but never seemed to know where they were going. But employers who had pistol-whipped Wobblies out of town had no more charitable reaction to more sensible union men with sensible ideas. In the harsh world of labor organization there was no substitute for power and little power without violence. So I accepted the ground rules of those days. I believed in militancy—if it meant that militancy would spur the labor movement along. Militancy was the same to me as artillery was to the field general. Our Teamsters could take care of themselves on practically any picket line."

During the bitter jurisdictional battles of the Thirties, Beck's organizing forces gathered together an army of what became known in the parlance of newspaper reporters as "goons."

Throughout the years, the Teamsters' pressure on their adversaries never relaxed. Laundries formed an employers' association to police their industry and appointed Bill Short, a friend of Beck's, to run it. Drivers within the jurisdiction of the Teamsters throughout the Pacific Northwest were organized.

John Francis Dore, in his legal capacity as attorney for the United Brewery Workers of America, fought Beck in a jurisdictional battle. Later, when Dore ran for mayor of Seattle against Arthur Langlie and Bob Harlan, Beck put his Teamster support behind Dore and gained a very effective ally. "As long as I'm mayor," Dore promised, "I'm going to do all in my power to help the teaming unions." He kept his word, too.

Beck also silenced the carping of Seattle's newspapers. When the American Newspaper Guild, then in the A.F.L., struck Hearst's *Seattle Post-Intelligencer*, Beck came to the Guild's aid. Hearst ordered his writers to beat out virulently anti-Beck radio scripts. General Clarance B. Blethen, corpulent publisher of the *Seattle Times*, indignantly wrote a headline which ended with the ringing line: "How do you like the look of Dave Beck's gun? The shame of it!"

Beck's response was to sue the *Post-Intelligencer* and four radio stations for $550,000 and the *Times* for $250,000, then settled out of court for $15,000 and $10,000, respectively. It was the last time a Seattle newspaper ever spoke such harsh words about him.

On other fronts Beck was consistently victorious. At one Teamster convention during his struggle to stem Harry Bridges' invasion of Seattle, he cried: "If Bridges and his crowd want to make this thing an alley fight, the Teamsters will wallow with them in the gutter, and when it is all over, we will be on top." The Teamsters wallowed, and they came out on top.

The same remorseless tactics were used to attack A.F. of L. United Brewery Workers. Hired hands trailed U.B.W. beer drivers, beat them up, and wrecked their trucks. Despite innumerable lawsuits, Beck also maintained a blockade which kept the opposition's California and eastern-made beer out of Seattle and Portland for many months. In the end every brewery in the 11 western states signed Teamster contracts.

Beck defeats the breweries:

A number of the big brewers banded together and sued me for $2½ million. The background leading up to the suit was this. In defining the rights of its membership to organize, the Teamsters always had observed the constitutional law of the A.F.ofL. We never went in asking for brewery workers, coopers, engineers, or carpenters; we asked only for drivers and helpers, which was the allocated jurisdiction given to us by the A.F.ofL. The brewery workers refused to acknowledge our jurisdiction. Three times they were on the verge of being expelled from the A.F.ofL.

for refusing to recognize its constitution. Whenever threatened with expulsion for violating our jurisdiction, they assured Teamster president Dan Tobin that they would turn over a new leaf and abide by the law of the A.F.ofL. But now they went back on their promise, and Tobin just sat back and let the breach fester and fester.

Prohibition came along about then and lasted for a few years. Then it reached the point where it started to tumble. I wrote a letter to Tobin: "The Democratic National Party, in its platform, provides for the abolition of prohibition. It will be successful. Are you now going to organize your jurisdiction, allocated by the A.F.ofL., as belonging to the Teamsters?" Tobin wrote back and said, yes, he was. That's all I wanted to know. I told him I was going to organize Oregon and Washington, which, with Tobin's approval, I proceeded to do. The brewery workers hit the roof. They demanded that the breweries had to employ brewery workers as *drivers* and *helpers*, as well as inside personnel. I immediately notified a brewery operator in Seattle that he was in big trouble with the Teamsters if he bowed to the brewery workers' demands. I gave him an ultimatum: If Teamsters were not driving those trucks, we'd refuse to work for the brewery. Its beer could just sit there.

The brewery fought back by suing me. The case was heard in Seattle's federal court. The judge warned me that I had to put the drivers back to work at 10 a.m. the next day or else. I told him, "I didn't order them out and I won't order them back." I said I'd go to jail first—and I meant it, too. The judge got very stern with me. "Mr. Beck," he said. "If your drivers aren't back to work tomorrow morning, you'll go to jail." I said I'd appeal all the way to the Supreme Court. I knew the legal procedure, and I had good attorneys, too. I had George Vanderveer, who never walked away from a fight in his life. Sure, I knew the obstacles if I persisted in fighting the court. But you've got to find a way around such an order. I could name a hundred ways to do it. There's always a way around, *if* you're willing to make the necessary sacrifices. Of course, I never went to jail. The upshot was that the brewers lost the suit, signed those contracts, and dropped the suit against me.

I remember when we decided to organize the Yellow Cab drivers in Seattle. One of our executive officers' cars was parked over on Stewart Street and some punk came along and sprayed acid on it. I immediately called a mass meeting in the Eagles Auditorium. The building was packed. I went up on that stage and described the whole picture. I had Perry Gardner, the driver of the sprayed car, get up and explain what had happened. Then I told that audience, "By God, we're going out and organize Yellow Cab. There's nobody going to get away with this rough stuff. But, men, no violence. I do not want violence." They rushed out of there like sailors on leave. No sooner had I adjourned the meeting than a taxicab was turned upside down over on Union Street. Then a cab was rolled over down at Fourth and Pike, with three passengers trapped inside; down near Second and Yesler, same thing. Downtown Seattle was in an uproar. Taxis were being tipped over all over town. I was back in my office in the Security Building when Captain Hedges of the police department telephoned and said I had to do something about the violence. "There's panic in the streets," he said. "You've got to stop it." I asked him what he was talking about. I told him, "I don't know anything about it." And he said, "Well, all hell has broken loose, and I think you're behind it." I explained to the captain I'd ordered no violence. I said, "I didn't tell my men to do this stuff." Then the insurance companies notified Yellow Cab they were dropping their insurance if the rough stuff didn't stop. Within 72 hours we signed Yellow Cab to a contract. That ended the fighting. It never flared up again.

McCallum:

Even as Teamsters applied bone-cracking pressure on picket lines in their various battles, Beck was seeking more peaceful means of accomplishing his ends. When the Seattle Junior Chamber of Commerce daringly asked him to speak at one of their meetings early in 1937, Beck shouted: "There is no place in the Teamsters for communists or bolshevists. I am for the *capitalistic* system!" The young men were almost as surprised as if he had rolled up his sleeve and disclosed a tattoo of an angel.

A few weeks later, while Detroit, St. Louis, and Chicago were plagued with sit-down strikes, the Seattle Real Estate Board also called on Beck for a few words. "I stand unalterably opposed to the sit-down strike," he purred. "It is illegal seizure of property and will breed revolution." Almost immediately, Harry Bridges did Beck a good turn. He came to Seattle and predicted the eventual extinction of the employer. Said Beck, in rebuttal: "Some of the finest men I know are employers." Business in general and the Chamber of Commerce in particular responded to this wooing like bees to clover. Reluctantly, businessmen decided that unions had come to stay. They now felt, not so reluctantly, that it would be smart business to make peace with Dave Beck, a man with a reputation for standing by contracts.

As peaceful techniques began to work, Beck's beef squads vanished almost as magically as they had appeared. Beck declared himself the foe of strikes and promised to prevent them—a promise which went virtually unbroken right up through his retirement in 1957.

To Beck's opponents the agreements he made with businessmen were "sweetheart contracts," or sellouts to the bosses. To the employers themselves they usually seemed far from that. But good or bad, for Beck they had the sanctity of law, and he stood ready to mangle any local that tried to wriggle out of their terms.

"You put your name to that contract and I don't give a good goddamn how bad it turns out to be, you live up to it," he warned his people. "Because your word is the most valuable thing you've got.

"There were no finer Teamster contracts in America

than the terms of those contracts in Seattle," Beck recalls today. "The term 'sweetheart contracts' was simply propaganda. You still hear about sweetheart contracts today—and with no more truth than was the case 30 years ago."

8

A City's Best Friend

*"I hope the people some day realize what they had in
Dave Beck—and let go."*

Homer A. Post, 89,
noted teacher, 1978

O NCE feared, Dave Beck became a re-
spected leading citizen of Seattle, a process that was encouraged by his tireless leadership in worthy projects of all
kinds: war loan drives, gifts of athletic equipment to
soldiers, blood donations, fund raising for church campaigns, and the Associated Boys Club. A partial list of contributions by the union through Beck while he was president included: The Good Neighbor Fund, $16,000; Seattle
University, $5,250; Seattle Rebuilding Fund, $5,000; Seattle Pacific College, $3,000; Holy Names Academy, $5,000;
Ballard General Hospital, $2,100; University of Washing-
ton Students' Association, $1,250; Seattle Rotary Club,
$1,000; New Ryther Child Center, $1,000; Bellarmine Prep
(Tacoma), $24,200; and March of Dimes, $1,000. Total:
$59,800. Most of the money was given without fanfare.

"These were not large sums of money," Beck remembers. "There were bigger contributions. For instance,
$20,000 was given by us to refurbish the YWCA; another
$22,000 was donated to build a swimming pool for the YMCA;

93

and another $18,000 for the Veterans of Foreign Wars' building program; $30,000 was appropriated to build an enlisted men's club at Fort Lawton; $25,000 was donated for the purchase of a home on Fraternity Row for mothers visiting their sons at University of Washington—we gave it to them rent-free for the duration of World War II, and at the end of the war we sold it and put the money in our treasury fund for charitable purposes. During this period of time we also took a prime part of union labor's endorsement of the Good Neighbor Fund. There was nothing more important in the eyes of the Teamsters than to support charities."

Jack Gordon, general manager of the Restaurant Association of the State of Washington, Inc., recalls that in 1953 Dave Beck was advised that the Children's Orthopedic Hospital needed help in moving from Queen Anne Hill to its present location in Laurelhurst, off Sand Point Way.

"Mr. Beck sprung into action," Gordon said. "He went right to work organizing trucking firms and their business leaders—Teamster drivers of trucks, taxi cabs and ambulances—to move the entire hospital, furniture, patients, supplies, medical and surgical equipment in the time limit of 24-48 hours from one site to another. What's more, no child was endangered for lack of medical attention, and the hospital was able to function without interruption!"

Beck saved a number of local institutions from bankruptcy; perhaps the most discussed was St. Mark's Cathedral, a high society church in which many prominent weddings took place. St. Mark's had fallen behind on its mortgage payments. A recession had struck Seattle, and none of the more affluent members, singly or in groups, appeared willing to dig down into their pockets and fork over the needed cash. When foreclosure became imminent, Emil Sick called upon Joshua Green and Dave Beck and several other prominent businessmen to come forth and save the day. Emil Sick and Beck also headed up the fund-raising drive for construction of the Seattle-King County Blood Bank.

Beck's popularity rose dramatically. He sat on the state parole board, the Seattle Civil Service Commission, the University of Washington Board of Regents, becoming president of the board in his final year and spearheading the drive for one of the most sophisticated college hospitals in America, and a member of the Seattle Boxing Commission. By the end of 1946 even the *Seattle Times* could say, "Many are wishing that there could be more Dave Becks in the national labor picture."

When one pioneer businessman, noted for his hard-nosed cynicism and candor, was asked in Seattle what he thought of Beck, he replied, "I think the unions are getting too powerful and some of that power has gone to the leaders' heads."

"Dave Beck, too?" he was asked.

"I didn't say that," he said.

"Well, what about Beck?"

"I'm not sure it's healthy for Beck to have such power, but as long as it's available, we in Seattle are mighty glad it's in *his* hands."

Despite some enemies, Beck by now was being heralded as "Mr. Seattle," the city's leading citizen. He had made a major impact on the local economy. Somebody once sat down and figured out that Beck was personally responsible for bringing $100,000,000 in outside money into Seattle (Beck recently told me it was even higher than that). Several years ago, William Mullenholz, Comptroller of the International Brotherhood of Teamsters, went through the records for verification. The following letter was the result of his research:

When the complete story of Beck's financial dealings in the Pacific Northwest for the International Brotherhood of Teamsters is told, its scope is truly amazing. In a period of five short years, transactions totaling some $85,000,000 were channeled through various Seattle banks and mortgage loan institutions. Each of the purchases and sales resulted in a tidy commission to whom—Beck? Absolutely not, but rather to each of the firms handling the transactions, firms in which Beck had no interest whatsoever—financial or otherwise—$85,000,000! Think of it. What other single individual citizen of Seattle in as short a time benefited his community so well?

Moreover, due to the availability of Teamsters Union funds through Beck, many families in Seattle enjoy living accommodations heretofore denied them. Why? Because Beck had and still has faith in the future of his adopted hometown. To date, over $21,000,000 of Teamster Union funds represented by way of mortgage loans in homes and business enterprises that have done much to stabilize living and working conditions in the area.

Consider the money that flowed into Seattle from the East immediately after Dave Beck took office on December 1, 1952. Deposits in Indianapolis banks, which were not drawing a penny of interest, were close to $7 million in cash. In the period December 11 to December 29, there was transferred from the Indiana National Bank to the Seattle First National in excess of $6,271,000, and to the Peoples National Bank approximately $500,000. Again, on January 30, 1953, another $500,000 was placed in the Seattle First from Indianapolis banks, and a final $1,000,000 was brought to Seattle on July 1, 1953, closing out in their entirety all Indianapolis accounts. Thus, almost immediately after assuming office, Dave Beck enriched Seattle by more than $7,771,000, funds that otherwise would not have been available for use in the Pacific Northwest.

But that was not the end—not by any means. Deposits in Seattle Banks totaling more than $70,000,000 were made by the International Brotherhood of Teamsters in the five years after Dave Beck took over the presidency. He, alone, probably benefited the financial health of the City of Seattle more than any other citizen in its history.

But that's only part of the story. Government security purchases totaling almost $35,000,000 were made during the years 1952-56; purchases involving bills, notes, certificates, Federal International Credit Bank and Federal Home Loan Bank debentures—and all through Seattle banks. In the same period sales of such securities amounted to $48,00,000, almost all of which were handled by Seattle firms.

Another example of Beck's love affair with Seattle was the financing of homes. What this has meant to home-buying veterans only they can determine. How many vets could have afforded the down payment demanded by private enterprise or even by F.H.A.? How many today would be living in decrepit houses had their been no Dave Beck? The record shows 1,058. The purchasing of G.I. loans for the union was only one way in which Dave Beck assisted the residents of Seattle. Before even a shovel touches the ground or hammer strikes a nail and before the sound of saw buzzing through wood begins, financing of construction must first be guaranteed. So Dave Beck made available interim construction money in the amount of $8,678,000. This was over and above all other enterprises. Three entire suburban housing developments are in existence today, thanks to Dave Beck.

But housing for veterans was not the only method in which the Seattle area profited from Beck's financial operations. First trust loans, to other than veterans, for housing, to small businesses, and to at least one hospital, all totaling some $2,600,000, were made in the years 1954-1957. The monies that were loaned to people in the Seattle area by virtue of Dave Beck's office amounted to nearly $21,000,000.

Nor was Seattle the only city on the West Coast to get Beck's attention. The veterans of World War II and the Korean war in the San Francisco area felt the touch of his hand by means of mortgage loans amounting to $1,600,000, while Los Angeles vets received loans of more than $5,000,000, besides first trusts of $400,000. As far south as Phoenix, Arizona, Teamster money was invested in G.I. loans in 1956-57 to the extent of over $800,000. All in all, 1,727 veterans on the West Coast got housing loans made available through the Dave Beck program.

Many businessmen up and down the coast grew to like Dave Beck. They did not forget that during the depression he had made the rounds of the local Teamster unions and convinced the members to take a cut in wages. Nobody had ever heard of such a thing. "I barely got out of some of those union halls with my head on," Beck laughs today. "But when business started to pick up, I saw to it that the cuts were restored."

On December 3, 1952, some 700 business leaders from throughout the State of Washington gathered at the Olympic Hotel in Seattle to honor Dave Beck's election as president of the International Brotherhood of Teamsters. Cochairmen were the publishers of the *Seattle Times* and of the *Post-Intelligencer*. Master of ceremonies was Brewer Emil Sick, chief beneficiary of the Beck-directed union war of the Thirties, when Beck permitted "not a single drop" of Brewery Workers Union beer to enter the Pacific Northwest from California or the East. Cried Sick: "We respect Dave Beck as a labor leader—the greatest in the United States."

Fellow Teamster leaders expressed their feelings for Beck in the preface of a brochure that was placed at each guest's plate:

A small, red-haired boy with freckled face was asked by his grade school teacher to write the following sentence in his tablet:

"He who hesitates is lost."

One hundred times this boy scribbled till his fingers felt numb. It was a sort of punishment for a minor classroom infraction. And how that grade-school boy remembered this important little lesson!

Certainly, had Dave Beck, the general president of the International Brotherhood of Teamsters, hesitated, we, the Teamster associates honoring him tonight, would have been the losers. In Dave Beck's book, hesitation is the mark of no confidence. "Think a problem through and through," says Dave, "but once you arrive at your decision, never waver." This has been his guiding light for the 34 years he has served as a member and leader in the Teamsters organization. The lessons he learned long ago, plus the legion of friends he has gained in our local organizations, have stood him well in his climb to the top. And Dave Beck never forgets his friends.

Tonight marks the fulfillment of a dream which started the first day he climbed aboard that laundry truck and started on his rounds. We all know the story because many of us started with him, others joined in his fight for right. Some have fallen, but none are forgotten.

Dave is a man's man, a sportsman, and a kindly man. He loves a joke as well as he loves a job well done. He has come far and our friendship and loyalty to him as our trusted leader have stood us well.

It was a night to remember. The roast beef was delicious, the champagne sparkled, and the speeches were laudatory. There was only one sour note:

Dave Beck was not there.

Beck relates the reasons for his absence:

Previous to the banquet, I attended a conference at the Lake Huron, Michigan, vacation place of Roy Fruehauf, head of the Trucking Association of the eastern area. We had been discussing some upcoming labor contract negotiations. That evening I was not feeling so hot and I retired early. Around midnight I started getting these excruciating sharp pains in the lower part of my back. I knew what they were; I was having an attack of kidney stones. Thinking there was no doctor within 250 miles, I tossed and turned all night, suffering. A day-long trip was scheduled for early morning, and at 6 o'clock here came the wake-up call. I told Roy I couldn't possibly go; that I was having a kidney attack and was in terrible pain. Roy asked me, "Well, why didn't you shout for us during the night?" I said, "There was no sense waking you up; I must get to a doctor." And Roy said, "Hell, Dave, there's one sleeping right next door to you." I hadn't known that.

Arrangements were quickly made for me to be flown to Washington, D.C., on the Fruehauf private plane. I was then taken to a hospital and examined. The doctor who conducted the examination said he had no choice but to operate. That was in contradiction to what my personal physician, Dr. Alexander Grinstein, was always telling me. "Never let them operate, if at all possible," he often said. So I phoned Dr. Grinstein in Seattle and, being the sort of friend he was, he caught the next plane to Washington. Alone in my hospital room, we discussed my condition. Dr. Grinstein confirmed what he was always advising me: no operation. Then the other doctor came in and the two of them talked. When we were alone again, I said to Dr. Grinstein, "But you never mentioned to him that you are against the operation." Dr. Grinstein said, "Dave, I can't tell him what to do. You're his patient. I don't practice medicine in Washington, D.C."

"The hell with that," I said.

When Dr. Grinstein left the room, I phoned the other doctor and canceled the surgery, which I was scheduled for the following morning. He didn't like it, but I was determined to get back to Seattle.

When we boarded the plane, Dr. Grinstein gave me a hell of a shot to kill the pain; he gave me another bang when we landed at Chicago; and another at Denver. Finally, just before we touched down at Seattle-Tacoma International Airport, I said to Dr. Grinstein, "Get me in shape for that banquet tonight."

"Banquet?" he said. "Who said anything about you going to a banquet?"

"I've got to go. They've been planning it for months," I said.

"No," he said.

"But more than 700 people are coming."

"I don't care," he said. "The only place you're going is to the hospital. You are a very sick man."

I begged, I pleaded, I cajoled—but Dr. Grinstein wouldn't give an inch. I told him, "All I want is to make a brief appearance, to thank all those people for honoring me."

"Forget it," Dr. Grinstein said, and that was that.

So the banquet went on without the guest of honor.

And—wouldn't you know it, at 11 o'clock the next morning I passed that damn stone.

McCallum:

Which was how Dave Beck missed the biggest celebration the City of Seattle ever held for Dave Beck.

Several years afterward, when the new International Union headquarters in Washington, D.C. were dedicated, Dave Beck was paid tribute by business and government leaders from all over America. One of those honoring him was Eric Johnston, a leader in the motion pictures industry and past president of the U.S. Chamber of Commerce. He turned to Beck with some unblushing doggerel:

> *If I had a key to heaven*
> *And you didn't have one, too,*
> *I'd throw away my key to heaven*
> *And go to hell with you.*

Beck:

Eric Johnston, from Spokane, and I were very close personal friends. Once he went to Dan Tobin and tried to hire me away from the Teamsters. Eric in his position within the motion picture industry wanted me to work for him. My salary was about $15,000 a year in those days, I don't remember, but Eric went to Tobin in Indianapolis and told him he wanted to make me an offer of $50,000 a year. Tobin threw up his hands, and said, "Whew! I can't pay Dave that kind of money. I don't want him to leave, yet I can't stand in his way either." So Eric came back to me and offered me a 10-year contract with a starting salary of $50,000. I told him, "Eric, I appreciate your offer, but you are wasting your time." "Dave," he said, "I cleared it with Tobin. He said he doesn't want you to leave, but he won't stop you." And I said, "You're still wasting your time, Eric. If you offered me $100,000, I wouldn't take it. Hollywood ain't for me, Eric. I'm in labor for life."

My logic was plain. I told Johnston, "I'd be a hypocrite if I went to work for you." He said he didn't understand. "Well," I said, "as you described the job, I'd be an adviser to you, primarily as it relates to your labor problems in the movie industry." "Yes, that's right," he said. "Well," I told him, "how the hell can I advocate the philosophy of labor one day, and turn around and argue for the other side the next? The only advantage in going with you is the money. I sure as hell would be making a lot more money—but I'm not interested in that."

Later, Skouras, one of the big studio heads, made a similar offer to me—a 10-year contract, $50,000 salary— and I gave him the same answer I gave Eric.

The studio bosses saw a lot of me in the 1930s and '40s. While I was organizing Los Angeles, I was in and out of town week after week, month after month. Seattle didn't see much of me. It got pretty rough in L.A., I can tell you. My safety wasn't worth a plugged nickel. That's the way it was in the early years of the labor movement. There were times when I was registered simultaneously at four or five different hotels in L.A. under four or five different names—none of them my own.

Bodyguard? No, I never had a bodyguard with me in my life. I never felt I needed one. Yes, I received crackpot notes and telephone threats. Lots of times. But I never hired a bodyguard, never packed a gun, and didn't even ask for a gun permit. The only time I was ever concerned was when the FBI phoned to warn me that a pair of parolees were on the way from Kansas to kidnap my son. Other than that instance, I took the threats all in stride. My philosophy was, it goes with the job.

It's interesting about Emil Sick. Not many people remember I put him in baseball. It all started when George Vanderveer, my attorney, came to me with a business proposition years ago. Bill Klepper owned the old Seattle Indians (Pacific Coast League) and George was his financial angel. Attendance was down and the ball club kept getting deeper and deeper in red ink. George was losing a small fortune. One day he called me. "Dave," he said, "do you like baseball?" "I love it," I said. "Well," he said, "come on over to my office. I have an interesting proposition for you." The first thing he said to me as I strolled into his office was, "Do you *really* like baseball?" "I sure do," I said. "Well, then," he said, "you own the Seattle ball club." I said to him, "What the hell are you talking about? You must be crazy, George. Why, I couldn't meet the first payroll—and I know you're not exactly getting rich with the club."

Frankly, the Indians were in terrible shape. Why would I want to saddle myself with them? A short time before, the old ball park in Rainier Valley had burned down, and they were playing their games at the Civic Auditorium, not precisely the best site in the world.

"Who the hell said anything about selling the ball club to you?" George continued. "I'm *giving* it to you. I'll give you all the financial support you need until the club gets back on its feet."

"Uh, uh, George," I said. "You can't even give it to me. I'm too busy organizing the Teamsters."

One word led to another. Finally, I said, "Why don't you have a talk with Emil Sick? Better yet, I'll talk to him for you. Let me see what I can do."

I grabbed my hat and walked up the street to Second and Marion, where Emil had his office. Emil and I were very close. I had stood by him, renewing his license, and putting him back in business at a time when the brewery workers tried to destroy his brewery. That really cemented our friendship. I never walked away from him, and he was always in my corner. So I told him about the Seattle ball club, pointing out what a valuable asset it could be for advertising his beer. Nobody has ever accused me of being shy, and by the time I walked out of Emil's office, the Indians had a new owner and a new name, the "Rainiers." He paid George something over $100,000 for the team, lock, stock and barrel; George got the Shell gas station on the corner adjoining the ball park.

That's how Emil Sick got into baseball; that's how I didn't. It was the beginning of a new era for baseball in Seattle. Emil built beautiful Sick's Stadium, hired Torchy Torrance as his promotion director, and in 1939-40-41, led the minor leagues in paid attendance with 500,000-plus each year. In those days that added up to a lot of suds.

McCallum:

Professionally, Beck reached his zenith with the dedication of the multimillion dollar International Teamsters headquarters in Washington, D.C. Prior to that magic hour, however, Dave traveled to other cities making speeches at Teamster dinners. Militance, as always, was his theme. "It is as if he fears that the new building, his pride and joy, might lead the rank and file to get the notion that the Teamsters have gone soft and political," commented one reporter. Pounding the lectern, Beck shouted: "We have always been a fighting union. We must never lose our alertness or go soft in the gut or we won't be worth a damn." In another city, he told his underlings, "We're well off, and we belong to the national picture and our new headquarters proves it. We're proud of being well off, but remember that we're not going to get fat and lazy."

As the nation's No. 1 cross-country commuter, Beck flew from Seattle to Washington (via New York, where he stayed in the Waldorf Towers "right next to General Mac-Arthur") to personally take charge of the dedication of the new Teamsters building. He was now confiding in the press corps that it had cost "somewhere between $5,000,000 and $6,000,000." Judging by its marble halls, plush carpets, and most modern of office equipment, no one argued with that estimate.

Parallel with the dedication was a lavish variety show to be staged in Constitution Hall for Teamster delegates and their families. Beck had thought of everything. It was a complete theatrical production featuring Scat Carruthers, the Tokayers' famous acrobatic act, and singers such as the Demarco Sisters, the Nota Belles, Earl Wrightson, Joan Holloway, Anne Crowley, and Margaret Whiting. Nor was there just one master of ceremonies to keep the show moving. There were *five*: Dan Dailey, Jack Haley, George Murphy, Pat O'Brien, and Walter Pidgeon.

Somebody had the nerve to ask Beck if five MCs wasn't a bit too pretentious. "What the hell," he snapped. "They're not here just as stars. They all belong to the A.F.ofL. They are here as unionized professional people in sympathy with the Teamsters. I'll make that clear."

The stars donated their services, too.

The Hollywood luminaries fell into the spirit of the evening. Walter Pidgeon told how he had been called in years past by both Tobin and Beck and said he was always happy to respond. In a burst of Irish sentiment Pat O'Brien told the Teamsters: "You are a wonderful people. I love you—God bless you!"

As the show reached its climax, the stars lured Beck onto the stage, where O'Brien grabbed him and danced him around. Then Margaret Whiting coaxed him into a duet. For Dave Beck, it was a night to remember.

Beck:

How do I close off this chapter without sounding like a bragger? I'm not asking for applause. What I did for my community, I did because I sincerely wanted to. Prestige wasn't part of it. Money wasn't part of it; money never meant much to me, contrary to what my critics say. I think my oldest friends will vouch that from the days they first knew me, when I didn't have a dime, I was always generous. Yes, I very definitely consider myself a generous person. Hell, I am not saying that to pat myself on the back, but as a poor kid from a poor family, I saw poverty from the inside. After I struck it rich, I simply wanted to put back into society some of that which I took out. I loaned out thousands of dollars—as much as $8,000 per to friends of my son back from the war. I helped four or five of them buy their homes and told them, "When your second child is born, I'll cancel the debt." In three instances, I did, too. Sure, I was generous with my money, and I still am. Shucks, I'll always want to be generous.

I advocated the labor movement giving to charities. I raised hundreds and hundreds of thousands of dollars for charities of every kind and character. The City of Hope, for example. I think I was the first one to go out and really put it on its feet. This is how I got involved. One of the insurance executives who was carrying our insurance walked into my office with the secretary of the union. He announced that he wanted to give me a third interest in his company. "Don't be ridiculous," I told him. "Don't discuss it any further." He said, "But, Dave, we're making a lot of money. You can be of great value to us." That riled me up. I said, "If you're making so much money, why don't you give to the City of Hope the third you are offering me?" By damn, he hadn't thought of that. So that's what he did. They got thousands and thousands of dollars out of him. I never took 15 cents, and I never wanted it.

Actually, when it came to money, I was quite conservative. I liked horse racing, but I never was a steady goer. Oh, I made a bet on the horses occasionally, but I was never what could be termed a gambler. I never played a game of cards in my life. Even as a kid, my friends would be playing pool, or shooting craps, or deep in a game of poker, and I'd be sitting off in a corner reading a book.

Looking back on my career, I have made many close friends, inside as well as outside of labor. Despite all the fighting that was directed against me by Seattle's business community and the State of Washington, I don't think there's a single person, right now, who has any more friends in Seattle business than Dave Beck. That has to say something about me.

9

Bitten by the Boston Terrier

A FRIEND of mine, whose sister once worked for Bobby Kennedy and believed in him passionately, said of him: "As far as my sister's concerned, after God, comes Bobby." To which his wife corrected, "You mean, after *Bobby*, comes God."

Robert F. Kennedy was a complicated man. It was almost impossible to generalize about him, and at the same time, it was almost impossible to feel neutral about him. Dick Schaap, the author and former city editor of the old *New York Herald Tribune*, once wrote of him: "Bobby inspires only the most forceful reactions. His friends, in their analysis, elevate him to the brink of sainthood; his enemies, in turn, condemn him to the inner circles of hell." Even the people who felt ambivalently about him expressed their ambivalence in the strongest possible terms, offering him, simultaneously, the ultimate in acceptance and the ultimate in rejection. "I'd sleep with him," said one woman reporter who had observed him often, "but I wouldn't vote for him."

Even the simplest, most elementary facts about Robert Kennedy ignited vastly differing interpretations. He could be judged ruthless or compassionate, brash or shy, detached or involved, devious or honest, opportunist or idealist, vacuous or intelligent. He was a flurry of contradictions. "Just when you get Bobby typed as the white hope, he'll do something so bad it'll jar you completely, destroy your faith in him," said a veteran newspaperman who had known him well for more than a decade. "And just as you're ready to accept the excessive condemnations, to accept him as ruthless and diabolical, he'll do something so classy it stuns you. He is very paradoxical."

The anti-Bobby voices did not trust him. Lacking trust, they doubted his motives, and by finding him opportunistic, devious, insincere, they called him a false liberal. Asked to present an indictment of him, they reached back to the influence of his father's fabulous wealth, to his service for and his friendship with Senator Joseph McCarthy, to his ruthless crusade against Dave Beck and Jimmy Hoffa and the Teamsters Union, starting in 1956.

The way Clark R. Mollenhoff and Thomas B. Morgan, a couple of investigative reporters for *Look* magazine, told it, Beck's troubles with Bobby Kennedy and the government began on August 1, 1956. Until then, Beck was generally regarded as the biggest labor boss in America.

That afternoon, Maxine Buffalohide, one of RFK's secretaries, finished typing a report for him. He was then 31 and the chief counsel for the Permanent Investigations Subcommittee of the United States Senate Committee on Government Operations. Handing the report to Bobby, Maxine asked for the rest of the afternoon off. "I'm all caught up," she told him. "There's nothing more to do." Bobby, noting her cleaned-off desk, said half-jokingly, "It looks like I'll have to find some new projects to keep you busy."

A reporter from *Look*, who had dropped in to talk about investigations with Bobby, spoke up; "This might be a good time to take on something tough, like an investigation of the Teamsters."

"I don't know if that's in our jurisdiction," Bobby said. "The Senate Labor Committee usually covers that field."

"Let's talk about it anyway," the reporter said. Kennedy and the reporter went into Bobby's office. Maxine Buffalohide didn't get the afternoon off.

Six weeks later, on October 15, Mollenhoff and Morgan recalled that late that morning Dave Beck had a private meeting with President Dwight D. Eisenhower at the White House. Ike was running for re-election. They shook hands. The photographers' flashbulbs made Beck blink and rub his pale blue eyes. Afterwards, a big smile clung to his lips. He was at the pinnacle of his career, "the businessman of labor," as some editorialists labeled him. As he left the White House, a few moments later, Beck bestowed his political blessings on the President. This *was* news. Beck made the front page of the *New York Times* the next morning, as well as all the other leading papers across the country.

Another five weeks passed. The morning of November 26 found Bobby Kennedy behind his desk, telephone in hand. He had just dialed STerling 3-0525, a local number. "Hello," he said. "May I speak to Einar Mohn?" Einar Mohn was the 50-year-old administrative vice-president of the Teamsters. His office was near Beck's in the $5,500,000 marble and glass Teamsters headquarters at 25 Louisiana Avenue. The building was across the Capitol plaza from the Senate Office building.

Mohn came to the phone. "Yes?" he said.

"This is Robert Kennedy. The Senate Investigations Subcommittee has begun an investigation of three of your vice-presidents and it wants your cooperation."

Mohn wanted to know if Beck was also under suspicion.

"No."

Kennedy assumed that millionaire Beck would not be

tempted by the $35,000,000 in the Teamsters' treasury.

Kennedy did not get an opportunity to explain the full purpose of his phone call. Mohn suddenly became belligerent. After more angry words, he hung up. If there was corruption in the Teamsters, Mohn certainly didn't give Kennedy the impression he wanted to help clean it up.

Kennedy decided to fly out to Portland, Oregon, and spend two days surveying Teamsters affairs there. Then he flew 160 miles north to Seattle and registered at the Olympic Hotel. For three days he tried to get in to see Beck, but Beck was unavailable. He did talk to an informant on the affairs of Frank Brewster, however. The informant insisted that Brewster, boss of the Western Conference of Teamsters, was up to his hips in corruption and for Kennedy to look into it.

Beck:

Bobby never would reveal who his informant was, but the guy also tried to implicate me. He told Bobby I was milking thousands of dollars from Teamsters' union funds, some of which even had been used in part payment for the construction of my home at 16749 Lake Shore Drive in suburban Seattle. That house provoked a lot of controversy. *Look* magazine quoted me as saying to one of its reporters: "The whole layout cost $85,000. That's conservative. A lot of wholesale went into it. You couldn't do it for twice that amount." By the time Bobby Kennedy had arrived in Seattle, I had sold the house to the Teamsters. Then the Teamsters turned the place back to me rent-free. Judged by an article in *Look*, writers Mollenhoff and Morgan made the transaction sound tainted. That just wasn't so. As president of the union, I was entitled to live in any residence of my choosing rent-free. First, I was offered Dan Tobin's place in Miami Beach, but I rejected it. I was also entitled to live in the house at Cape Cod, outside Boston, that the Teamsters owned. That, too, was out of the question, because my wife wanted to live in Seattle. The Teamsters' executive board said, well, where did I want to live, in what house, and I said I wanted to keep the place at 16749 Lake Shore Drive. They said, fine, they'd buy it from me, then let me live in it rent-free, and that's what they did. I owned the house, I had built it. I'd built it long before I was elected general president of the Teamsters.

When I retired as president and Jimmy Hoffa replaced me, he could have lived in the house. But he didn't want to live in the Pacific Northwest. His roots were in the Midwest. I suppose if I'd wanted to bid for the house I could have bought it back from the Teamsters. The truth is I didn't want it. It was too big for just my wife and me. So the Teamsters placed it on the open market and sold it. They got $85,000 or $90,000 for it, after paying me $137,000 originally. Why would they sell it for nearly $50,000 less than they paid for it? Your guess is as good as mine. I advised them against it, but they sold it anyway. Today, the place is valued at a round $240,000, and the German Consul is renting it on a 10-year lease at $20,000 a year.

McCallum:

Bobby Kennedy smelled blood. The 31-year-old lawyer had the true prospector's instinct for the jugular. Now he was in hot pursuit of the bosses of the powerful Teamsters. He was full of tricks. Armed with supreme self-confidence and an initial appropriation of $350,000, Kennedy sent his staff legmen into a dozen cities. While Bobby, himself, was in Seattle he talked to an Army corporal who passed on idle chitchat from a girl he met at a dance. The soldier said that the girl worked as a maid for a woman employed by the Teamsters; under the woman's bed was a stack of their records. Anxious to get his hands on any Teamster files, Bobby got the corporal to continue dating the maid. He also arranged to have a member of his staff accompany them and the maid's girl friend on a double date. Capping the evening at the Teamster employee's home, the corporal kept the girls amused while Kennedy's investigator feigned illness, staggered to the bedroom for a quick look at the records under the bed.

Working 17-hour days, Kennedy hopped back and forth across the country drawing together the findings.

On December 17, Kennedy arrived in Chicago, where he managed to talk to Nathan Shefferman, who was the director of a company called Labor Relations Associates, Inc. The concern was dedicated to helping labor see management's point of view. Kennedy's informer back in Seattle claimed that Beck and Shefferman had had business dealings. In his office at 75 East Wacker, the white-haired Shefferman, 69, freely discussed his business with Beck. He admitted paying bills amounting to thousands of dollars for Beck: $991 for a rug, $14 each for ties, $43 apiece for Sulka shirts, etc.

"But Beck has always paid me back," Shefferman said.

"Do you know if the money comes from union funds?" Kennedy wanted to know.

"I don't know."

"Are there books?"

"Yes."

"May I see them?"

"My son, Shelton, has them. He's out of town, but he'll be back in two days. I'll deliver them to you then."

Nathan Shefferman kept his promise. From the records, such evidence was turned up as a slip showing that a check for $8,826.98 had been deposited to a Shefferman account. The check was traced to the Western Conference of Teamsters. Kennedy decided to turn the books over to Carmine S. Bellino, 50, former head of the FBI's accounting division and the subcommittee's chief accountant, for a full analysis.

After a week in the Midwest, Kennedy returned to Washington and called Senator John McClellan, chairman of the subcommittee.

"The Teamsters refuse to cooperate," Bobby told him. "They won't let us examine their financial records."

McClellan hit the roof.

"We'll see about that," he said. "I'll use all the muscle at my command to get those books."

Kennedy next phoned Teamster headquarters in an effort to track down Beck. He was informed that Beck would rather not be subpoenaed; he'd be willing to sit down and talk voluntarily. He had scheduled a business trip to Europe for early January and did not want a subpoena to interfere with it.

On January 3, attorney J. Albert Woll and other top Teamster officials met in Chicago to map out union strategy. It was decided to attack the jurisdiction of the McClellan subcommittee and to advise Teamster officers that if they use the Fifth Amendment, the union would not discipline them. "The committee will be stymied if no one talks," one of the strategists said.

Meanwhile, back in Washington, Beck was missing. No one could find him, including the subcommittee. Kennedy, armed with a subpoena, contacted United Airlines. Yes, there was a Mr. Beck booked on a January 4th flight from Seattle to New York. Mr. Dave Beck. Kennedy then telephoned attorney Woll.

"Where is Mr. Beck?"

"I don't know."

"Well," Kennedy said, "I know he's scheduled to fly from Seattle to New York."

"How do you know that?"

"I just talked to the airlines."

"All right, so he's in Seattle. What do you want him for?"

"Listen," Kennedy said. "If he doesn't want a subpoena, he'd better make himself available. It is important I talk to him."

"Meet me in the lobby of the Waldorf-Astoria tomorrow night at 9. I'll set up a meeting with Mr. Beck."

At 9 p.m. sharp, on January 5, Kennedy and Carmine Bellino met Woll at the Waldorf, and the three of them rode in silence to the 10th floor. Beck was registered in room 1003. For the first time, Kennedy and Beck stood face to face.

Beck:

The meeting lasted for about 90 minutes. I told Bobby that congressional investigators just didn't know how tough it was for me, as president of the Teamsters, to clean out the communists and racketeers, if there were any. I said I'd crucify any s.o.b. caught muscling or racketeering. As far as I was concerned, I told him, I'd done a pretty good job since December, 1952, when I was elected. "My mother didn't raise crazy children," I said. "I won't lie for anybody."

In talking to Kennedy, I denied knowledge of any wrongdoing in the Teamsters' union. I also refused to discuss my home in Seattle or my dealings with Shefferman. That was none of their business, and I told Bobby so. Then he handed me a letter from Senator McClellan. I put on my black-rimmed reading glasses and read it. McClellan made it clear that he planned hearings for mid-January and he expected me to be there. He warned that he was going to introduce evidence showing I'd "misused" Teamsters' union funds. I could feel my pink cheeks burning. It had been a long, long time since I had been slapped in the face with a flat charge of corruption. I put the letter down and stared at Bobby. He stared back, waiting for the thunder that never came. "You'll hear about this," was all I said. After all, Bobby Kennedy was not the only one in Washington with connections.

McCallum:

Dave Beck was a big wheel, make no mistake. He had thrice been offered the post of Secretary of Labor—by Roosevelt, Truman, and Eisenhower; had made the covers of *Time* (twice) and *Newsweek*, and was the subject of a full profile in *Life*. He knew everybody important in both political parties. He could eat lunch in the Senate restaurant with such men as Estes Kefauver or call on men of the caliber of Hubert Humphrey any time. Once, on a plane from San Francisco, California's Governor Goodwin J. Knight asked a reporter riding with Beck to sit in the rear so he could talk privately with Beck. Beck packed plenty of influence, no doubt about it. Kennedy and Bellino still had a long way to go.

On January 6, 1957, Beck boarded a plane in New York to fly to London for a meeting of the International Transport Workers Federation the next day. He was not under subpoena when he left. In fact, he had assurances from Chairman McClellan before leaving that it was perfectly all right to go. However, Senator McClellan later said he definitely told Beck to be back for the hearings, January 17, which Beck subsequently denied.

Beck:

Actually, what happened was this. I phoned Senator Scoop Jackson and asked him to call McClellan for permission for me to go to Europe. An hour later, Jackson phoned me back and said he'd talked to McClellan and McClellan told him I could go. I had planned the trip months in advance. I wasn't running from the McClellan hearings. That's absurd. I never ran away from a fight in my life. Besides, McClellan told Jackson he had no objections to my going.

Just before I left, I got a request from Bobby Kennedy, asking for a face-to-face meeting at the Waldorf-Astoria. I said, sure, let's talk. So I sat down with Bobby and somebody with him, I don't remember his name, and we talked for an hour and a half. I've already told you what we talked about, the threats he made to me. The next morning I flew over to Europe. At the time, the newspapers kept referring to me as "millionaire Beck." If I was a millionaire—and

I'm not sure that I was—every asset I had in the world then was tied up in Seattle. My son, my wife, my mother, everybody I loved or had any close relationship with, were all in Seattle. So I ask you, why in hell would I go to Europe with the idea of staying there, just to avoid the McClellan committee hearings? I had too much at stake here at home.

McCallum:

On the day the hearing on labor rackets opened, January 17, 1957, Bobby Kennedy got hold of a copy of a telegram that Einar Mohn had earlier sent out to various vice-presidents of the Teamsters, instructing them that they could "assert their constitutional or legal privileges" without fear of union disciplinary action. This included taking the Fifth Amendment. The policy stated in the telegram was a direct challenge to Chairman McClellan's subcommittee. (The policy also led to a new A.F.L.-C.I.O. position on the Fifth Amendment; that an official refusing to answer questions about union finances because he might incriminate himself should be expelled.)

It was a make-or-break moment for the whole investigation. Already, a jurisdictional fight was fomenting. It threatened to throw the entire probe into the sort of frustration that had nullified the work of various congressional committees from 1952 to 1956. No fewer than six committees of the Congress had meekly thrown in the towel heretofore. Was the McClellan committee going to be the seventh to fail?

Senator McClellan, despite the fact that no jurisdictional line had been drawn, went ahead with his first witness, Frank Brewster, the West Coast boss of the Teamsters. Boldly, Brewster took the Fifth Amendment on the ground that McClellan's committee had no jurisdiction. The pattern was thus established. In the next few days, Einar Mohn and fellow Teamsters refused to answer any questions. Meanwhile, Dave Beck did not appear.

Look magazine reported:

> On January 22, AFL-CIO President George Meany sent a letter to Labor Secretary James Mitchell containing two names from which the administration could name one representative to the International Labor Organization meeting in Hamburg, Germany, March 11-23. One was Harold D. Ulrich of Boston, a regional official of the Brotherhood of Railway Clerks. The other was Dave Beck.

Eight days later, Senator McClellan started action to cite Brewster, Mohn, and two others for contempt of Congress. He had told fellow senators of the telegram that Mohn had sent out to other Teamsters vice-presidents. McClellan claimed it had been sent out with Beck's blessings. "I can prove Beck's bad faith," McClellan told reporters. "Instead of coming before the committee, he remains in Europe."

In Europe Beck explained to reporters in almost daily interviews that he positively had not fled the U.S. to avoid appearing before the rackets committee. "I'm not evading the McClellan committee," he told the press. "I'm merely marking time over here until the I.L.O. meeting in Hamburg." On March 4, after a meeting with Senator McClellan, Secretary of Labor Mitchell wired Beck that the I.L.O. nomination had been withdrawn so that it would not interfere with Beck's return to the U.S. for any business he might have with the committee. Beck agreed to appear and testify on March 26.

"Beck will testify precisely as his lawyers advise him," wrote the *Newsweek* correspondent. "He will not risk a citation for contempt. However, he comes from a rough union; and some of his lieutenants probably will go to great lengths to avoid testifying—some already have pleaded the Fifth Amendment. For that reason, before the summer is over, the Teamsters will have to stand scrutiny before the ethical-practices committee of the combined A.F.L.-C.I.O. The committee will have the unhappy job of deciding whether to kick out of the American labor movement its most powerful single union. The chances are it won't dare. Dave Beck will remain the man who decides whether the wheels of America will go round."

On March 10, Beck returned to the U.S. and a week later sat in the hot seat of "Face The Nation," the CBS newspanel show, and told a national audience that, why sure, he'd borrowed between $300,000 and $400,000 interest-free from the Teamsters' treasury. So what?

Nine days afterward, on March 26, Beck finally took the witness chair before the McClellan committee. The Senate caucus room was jammed with press people, congressmen, and curious spectators. Beck wore a lightweight, gray, tailor-made suit, specially cut to cover the fact that "one shoulder is higher than the other from carrying newspapers when I was a kid." He was the picture of resplendent confidence. On his way into the caucus room a reporter had asked him, "Are you nervous?" And Beck said, "Nervous? Me? Haw!" Minutes later, he bellied up to the witness table for two days of testimony.

In an opening statement Chairman McClellan set the tone of the questioning. He said the committee had information indicating that "the president of the International Brotherhood of Teamsters, Chauffeurs, Warehousemen and Helpers of America, the largest and most powerful union in our country, may have misappropriated over $320,000 of union funds."

On the table in front of Beck was a brown leather briefcase bulging with the personal financial records that the committee had asked him to bring. But when ordered to turn them over, Beck unfolded a slip of white paper and began to read from it: "I must decline to do so because the committee lacks jurisdiction or authority under Articles 1, 2 and 3 of the Constitution, and, further, because my rights and privileges granted by the Constitution as supplemented by the Fourth and Fifth Amendments are violated."

McClellan was plainly frustrated. He leaned forward, frowned, and then pitched his next question: "The chair wants to know if you honestly believe that the submission of your records to this committee might tend to incriminate you?"

Beck had no doubts.

"Yes," he replied. "I think very definitely so."

During his appearance that first day, Beck was to drone out the prepared statement 65 times, although his natural combativeness often brought him perilously close to breaking the routine.

"Do you," asked Chairman McClellan at one point, "regard your privileges under the Fifth Amendment as transcending your duty and obligations to the laboring men of this country who belong to your union?"

Beck's face reddened, his head shot forward, his lips moved as he shaped an outraged reply. Just in time, Arthur Condon, his attorney, drove a sharp knuckle in to Beck's back. Three times Beck started to answer; three times Condon's knuckle dug into his spine. Every time Beck felt that knuckle, he fell back and automatically began reading, "I must decline . . . ."

After his first day, Beck, on his way out of the hearing room, told newsmen: "I'll be able to come out of this clean and white, one hundred percent!" Then he hurried across the grounds of the U.S. Capitol to the Teamsters' gleaming ($5,500,000) headquarters, closed the elevator door between himself and pursuing reporters, and rode up to his office on the third floor—a combination of glass, soft colors, and thick carpeting.

Beck sat down at his big walnut desk. At his fingertips was a panel of buttons; one of them connected him with a 27-inch Fleetwood television set. He flicked it on, then ate a steak dinner while watching kinescopes of his appearance before the McClellan committee.

At 8 o'clock he left the office and drove to the $450-a-month Woodner Apartments suite, on 16th Street in

Northwest Washington, which was maintained for his exclusive use, although he spent only three or four days a month in Washington, preferring, instead, to operate from his Seattle headquarters. Beck then conferred with his old friend and chief counsel, James Duff, the 74-year-old ex-Senator from Pennsylvania. Duff had stayed away from the hearings on the ground that it would be in poor taste for him to appear alongside Beck before his recent colleagues.

After phoning his wife, Dorothy, in Seattle, Beck went to bed early for a full eight hours' sleep.

Next morning there was a clanging overture to Beck's return appearance on the witness stand. The committee had called up Nathan Shefferman, the 69-year-old labor-relations consultant from Chicago. Shefferman's main business was representing employers in their dealings with organized labor. Obviously, Beck was a good man to know. Shefferman went out of his way to cultivate him.

"Isn't it true," Senator McClellan asked, "that in 1949-50 you made Mr. Beck a handsome gift of $24,500? Why?"

"Well, Mr. Beck, if you will permit me, is a terrific personality," Shefferman replied. "He is very attentive to his friends and very generous to his folks and people who surround him."

The room broke into loud laughter.

"Now, this is no laughing matter," Shefferman said, when order had been restored.

But laughing loudest of all was Beck, seated two rows behind Shefferman, and he kept grinning even while Shefferman admitted that he had acted as Beck's purchasing agent on items ranging from sheet roofing ($1,431) to a "thingamajig" for Dave Beck, Jr.'s camera. Haltingly, Shefferman reviewed the list of purchases: "Now, shirts, yes, he wears pretty good shirts; Coldspots and radios, golf balls. I don't think he plays golf, so he must be very generous and gave away the golf balls. Yes, and two silk shirts. Yes, and sheets and pillow cases, Bendix washer, football tickets . . . 21 pairs of nylons. Well, wait a minute, gentlemen. Please, the implication—I happen to know Mr. Beck is a moral man, and so it was perfectly all right. . . ."

Beck took the witness chair again. He was still not talking, even though he knew that George Meany, president of the A.F.L.-C.I.O., had moved to oust him from the A.F.L.-C.I.O. Executive Council "within 10 seconds after I heard him take the Fifth Amendment." About Shefferman's testimony, Beck continued to tell the committee, "I must decline . . . ."

Determined to place in the record the results of months of investigation, Committee Counsel Bobby Kennedy took the floor and outlined his chief case against Beck. He charged that from 1948 to 1953 Beck took $196,000 in Teamsters' funds to pay Contractor John Lindsay for work done on Beck's lakefront Seattle Compound. In March 1954, he said, Internal Revenue agents began looking into Beck's affairs—"And Mr. Beck decided he had better get things straightened out with his union." Beck, claimed Kennedy, went to the Fruehauf Trailer Co. of Detroit and asked to borrow $200,000. "The Fruehauf people were only too glad to oblige, since the Teamsters, at Mr. Beck's command, had lent the company $1,500,000 in 1953," Kennedy said. "But Fruehauf did not, in fact, have $200,000 it could spare, so its officers went to the Brown Equipment & Manufacturing Co., a tractor outfit in New York. Brown made four checks for $50,000 each, which were turned over to Mr. Beck. Then the Brown Company began pressing for repayment, and Mr. Beck had to come up with another solution. His solution was to sell his house to the union, which, of course, the union had paid for originally, or at least part of it. The price was $163,000, and Mr. Beck also got the right to live in that same home, rent-free."

Senator McClellan asked Beck if Kennedy had given a correct accounting.

"I must decline . . . ."

Beck's appearance before the McClellan committee was over. But before he could fly back to Seattle, he had first to listen to a parting shot from Counsel Kennedy: "I am not at all surprised to see Mr. Beck duck behind the Fifth Amendment. Yet with the records we have, we'll prove what he would have said if he had talked."

Beck:

Somebody figured out that I took the Fifth Amendment 142 times in reply to committee questions. "Why'd you plead the Fifth so often?" a reporter asked me afterward. I explained to him that it was all to keep from embarrassing politicians who got campaign contributions from the Teamsters. "If I did go ahead and talk," I said, "it might blow the lid right off the Senate." That quote in the papers made South Dakota's Republican Senator Karl Mundt, a member of the McClellan committee, fume. He threatened to call me back in again to substantiate my remark. But he never did; nothing more came of it.

Actually, it was upon the advice of my attorney that I took the Fifth Amendment. I had tax cases pending in the court and whatever I told the McClellan committee could later be held against me when my tax litigation case came up. Once I started answering questions, I'd have been wide open to everything. Don Duncan said he felt sorry for me when he watched me on TV during the hearings and Bobby Kennedy went into his act. "Those were the days when Bobby was rough and tough," Don said. "I don't mean he was right, but he was rough, tough and banker's-heart cold. I certainly, even totally innocent, would not want to be sitting across from him at a hearing in those days." It wasn't that bad. Kennedy didn't scare me. I only wish I could have taken off my gloves. I wish my attorney would have let me talk.

Kennedy tried to make a big scandal out of the Fruehauf thing. Sure, I borrowed $200,000 from Fruehauf. I gave notes for the loan. I paid every cent back with interest. The case was tried in two courts. At the first hearing, the judge instructed the U.S. attorney that before a trial of that sort starts, both the defense and the government are given opportunities to argue the defense's contention that the trial has no merit and should be dismissed. So they filed affidavits, and the judge gave them 30 minutes apiece to argue. Louis Nizer represented Fruehauf; Cyrus Vance, now the Secretary of State, represented the Brown Manufacturing Company; my attorney was Seattle's Charles Burdell. It was agreed that Nizer would represent all three of us in arguing why the case should be thrown out.

Nizer told the court that the transaction in question was nothing more than a simple loan. No one was absconding with funds; it was a *loan* which was paid back with interest. Nizer talked for about 20 minutes. There was no jury. The decision was left solely up to the judge. Then the government attorney was called to present its side of the case. After 25 minutes of waxing, the judge suddenly stopped him. "Just a minute," the judge told him. "You've been talking for 25 minutes. In the very first line of your written reply here—that which you are elaborating on now—you contend that it was a loan. Now, will you show this court where it was *not* a loan?" At the end of the allotted 30 minutes, the judge pounded his gavel, and said, "You still haven't proven to the court where it wasn't a loan. Why, even you, yourself, referred to it as a loan." Nizer then waived and gave the government attorney additional time to make this point. After another 15 minutes, down came the judge's gavel: "The issue in question was nothing but a *loan*. Case dismissed."

Bobby Kennedy refused to accept the defeat. The next thing we knew we were back in court. Because the case was the first of its kind ever, Kennedy took it directly to the U.S. Supreme Court. Now, what political action was necessary to get such fast action, I don't know, but that's where it went. "Fine, we'll send it to trial," the Supreme Court said. The trial was held in New York, and this time a jury heard it. The jury took only 25 minutes to return a verdict of not guilty. The case was dismissed and we all went home. That was the end of it.

For the record, in 1950, trucking management and the Teamsters set up a trade association to promote the industry through legislation and the like. Members included myself as chairman, Roy Fruehauf, president of the Fruehauf Trailer Co., and Bert M. Seymour, head of Associated Transport Co. When Roy Fruehauf faced a proxy fight in 1953 with George J. Kolowich, he came to me for help.

I told Roy Fruehauf to meet me for breakfast at the Waldorf-Astoria, where I was staying. He said he was bringing his attorney with him. The attorney's name was Landon, a leading corporation lawyer who specialized in the merging of companies. Landon was a big stockholder in Fruehauf Trailer Co. Instead of meeting them in the dining room, I went to Roy's room to pick him up to go to breakfast. Roy came to the door. I took one look at him and said, "My God, Roy, what's the matter with you? You look like hell."

"Dave," he said, "I'm going to lose my company. My brother and an associate from the Denver-Chicago Truck Lines are lining up options and buying stock. They're taking over the Fruehauf Corporation. I've been all over Wall Street trying to raise money to offset it, but the banks won't lend me a dime. The word is out not to do business with me. I've worn my shoes out trying to get the money."

He then confided in me how much stock that he, his wife, and Landon and his wife controlled. "All right, Roy," I said, "if the facts are as you say, and you're willing to give the Teamsters, or a designated agent, control of all stock that you, your wife, and the Landons own, I'll loan you $1½ million. We can draw up the papers tomorrow morning at 9 o'clock."

I then asked Landon if he was agreeable to my proposal. He said he was. So I telephoned my attorney back in Seattle, Simon Wampold, and instructed him to catch the next plane for New York, where he and Landon could sit down and hammer out the conditions of the loan. I told Roy and Landon that I wanted them to put every dollar of their stock in escrow with Walter Granger, of the New York Stock Exchange. "We deal only through Mr. Granger," I insisted. Walter Granger was a millionaire, a former Brown University football star, and a square guy.

Next day, the attorneys roughed out an agreement. But when they brought it to me for approval, I noticed they had scratched out one of my original provisions: that every dollar coming back in the form of dividends could not be delivered to Fruehauf Trailer Company, or used for the purchase of additional stock; that any profit arising from our loan must go to help pay off what Fruehauf owed us.

"Simon," I asked, "who took that paragraph out?"

"I did," he said. "It's entirely legal. There's no reason for it to be in there."

"Without that paragraph," I told him, "there will be no deal."

"Yes," he said, "but without it they can make a lot of money when the stock goes up."

"Forget it, " I said. "it's not my money—it's Teamsters' money. I insist you restore that paragraph."

Landon then spoke up (and he later testified under oath in court he said this):

"Dave, if you'll leave the contract alone, we'll siphon a big percentage of the profits over to you and you'll make $100,000 or $150,000."

I told him, "I don't care if you promise me a *million*, you're changing it back to my original proposal. I don't want it."

And the contract was rewritten to my specifications.

There was in existence an obscure Roy Fruehauf Foundation, Inc., established to train leader dogs for the blind. Fruehauf was its president. The foundation, and Roy personally, guaranteed the Teamsters a 4-percent return on the union's money, as well as full repayment. The loan was fully repaid by October, 1955, after turning out to be a good deal for everybody. Resultantly, Roy not only kept control of his company, but he bankrupted the Denver-Chicago Trucking Co. and ruined his brother and the other guy in the process.

Now, about that $200,000 loan I got from Fruehauf. I needed the money to make up a deficit on a loan I received from the Teamsters. Roy was happy to help me out; he turned over the money to the Brown Equipment & Mfg. Co., a subsidiary of Associated Transport, to give to me. When money grew tight and I couldn't pay Brown Equipment on time, Bert Seymour, president of Associated Transport, came to my aid by arranging for a loan from the Manufacturers Trust Co. of New York. Finally, in April, 1955, I paid off Brown Equipment (with interest) by selling my home to the Teamsters for $163,000 in a perfectly normal transaction that Bobby Kennedy tried to turn into a scandal.

A lot of smoke was also made out of my dealings with Shefferman; smoke, yes, but not fire. He was a wheeler-dealer, knew how to get purchases wholesale. With Sears Roebuck, for example, he often got discounts of as much as 25-30 percent below the retail price. He used his connections to do favors for a lot of prominent people. He did the same things for Walter Reuther that he did for me. But what discount goods I got from him, I always paid out of my own funds, not the Teamsters'. There was no International money involved. Shefferman got no favors from me at any time in his life. Never! Nobody else did, either, when it came to Teamster business.

McCallum:

In April, 1957, several weeks following his appearance before the McClellan committee, Beck showed up at the Galvez Hotel in Galveston, Texas, where he was on hand to attend a meeting of the Teamsters' General Executive

Board. He repeated to newsmen that "this whole damn business doesn't bother me a damn bit," meaning the Senate investigation. When it came time to go into the closed-door General Executive Board meeting, he seemed almost eager to face the fireworks. Five hours later he bounced out beaming. The General Executive Board had resolved that (1) the A.F.L.-C.I.O.'s suspension of him as an A.F.L.-C.I.O. vice-president was "illegal," and (2) the Teamsters would refuse to appear before the A.F.L.-C.I.O. Ethical Practices Committee "on May 6, 1957 or at any other time" until they got guarantees of a "fair" hearing.

Tough-minded George Meany was unimpressed. In his prompt retort to the Galveston resolutions, Meany made it clear that united labor would go ahead and pass judgment on the Teamsters whether they showed up to defend themselves or not.

"The only accuser of Mr. Beck," said Meany, "will be Mr. Beck—his own testimony, his lack of testimony, and the record."

Meanwhile, the 10-strike bowled by the McClellan committee against the Teamsters Union had labor leaders everywhere picking up the splinters. Such as:

In Washington, James G. Cross, president of the Bakery and Confectionery Workers Union (160,000 members), announced that he would repay the union for personal phone calls, which a rival union official said amounted to some $2,400. What's more, he promised to return the new Cadillac that came to him as a "gift" from another union official.

In New York, David Dubinsky, president of the International Ladies' Garment Workers Union (450,000 members), set out to demonstrate that labor could clean its own house by appointing himself as a one-man jury and judge for union officials and staffers who had taken $100 to $500 gifts from employers. He warned that the penalties would be harsh.

In Atlantic City, where the United Auto Workers were

attending their biennial convention, President Walter Reuther named a "public watchdog" committee to oversee U.A.W. ethics.

The clean-up was on.

Beck:

On May 6, 1957, I sat before the A.F.L.-C.I.O. Ethical Practices Committee. Meany had promised a fair hearing. Hogwash! I no sooner was settled in my chair than he started to ask me the same questions I'd been asked by the Senate committee. On the advice of my attorney, I looked straight at Meany and asked: "Will you guarantee me that if I answer these questions—and I'm perfectly willing to level with you—they won't be subpoenaed by the Senate? Give me that guarantee now and I'll tell you anything you want to know."

Meany's face turned lobster-red with ire. He knew damn well he couldn't give me such assurance.

"You can't do it," I told him. "You have no authority; you're going through the back door instead of the front door."

A month later, Meany suggested that I be removed from the Teamsters Executive Council of the A.F.L.-C.I.O. even before my term ended in September.

Of course, Meany finally got his way and the Teamsters were expelled from the A.F.L.-C.I.O. They knocked us down, flattened us, but the important thing to remember is that, like a good fist-fighter, we didn't stay down. We got back up, dusted ourselves off, and grew bigger than ever. We are the one international union that continues to grow. We proved conclusively, I think, that we had a powerful union, properly officered, with splendid membership—and our critics be hanged. Sure, we have our faults, plenty of them, but we're a human family. But, all considered, I think we did a tremendous job proving to the world we don't need the American Federation of Labor.

Dave Beck Elected New Teamster President

Seattle Post—Intelligencer

Telephone, MAin 2000   18 PAGES   Main Office—6th Ave. and Wall St.

VOL. CXLIII, No. 49   SEATTLE, SATURDAY, OCTOBER 18, 1952

SPORTS SPECIAL

DAVE BECK SUCCEEDS DAN TOBIN— Seattle's Dave Beck got a friendly pat on the head from the man he succeeded Friday as president of the American Federation of Labor International Brotherhood | of Teamsters, Daniel J. Tobin. Tobin stepped aside after 45 years as head of the union of 1¼ million members. Beck was elected by acclamation at the union's convention in Las Angeles.

SEATTLE MAN **Ike Attacks Truman**
SUCCESSOR TO **On Civil Rights Vote**
DANIEL J. TOBIN NEWARK, N. J., Oct. 17.—(INS)—Gen. Dwight Eisenhower tonight bitterly attacked President Truman's record on civil rights and said he will use his influence as President to try to get every state to pass . . .

Dave Beck (left) with Daniel J. Tobin immediately after Beck was elected president of the International Brotherhood of Teamsters in 1952. Tobin had headed the Teamsters for 45 years.

Dave Beck and friend. Beck was offered the position of Secretary of Labor by Presidents Roosevelt, Eisenhower and Truman. He declined all three offers to remain a part of the labor movement.

Margaret Whiting, singer, and Jack Haley, actor, helped Dave Beck and others dedicate the new Teamsters International headquarters in Washington, D.C., 1955.

Executive Board of the International Brotherhood of Teamsters, Chauffeurs, Warehousemen and Helpers of America. The year is 1952. Dave Beck had just been elected president. Standing, left to right: James Hoffa, Thomas Hickey, Harry Tevis, Einar Mohn, Joseph Diviny, Frank Brewster, William Lee. Seated left to right: Sidney Brennan, John Murphy, John English, Dave Beck, John Conlin, John O'Brien.

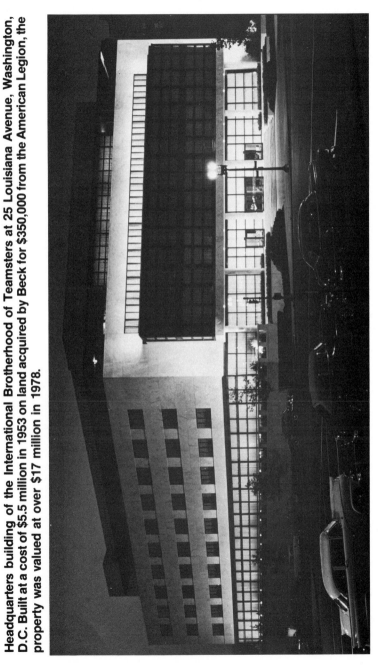

Headquarters building of the International Brotherhood of Teamsters at 25 Louisiana Avenue, Washington, D.C. Built at a cost of $5.5 million in 1953 on land acquired by Beck for $350,000 from the American Legion, the property was valued at over $17 million in 1978.

Dave and Dorothy Beck on the balcony of the new Teamsters head-quarters building in 1955 at the dedication of the new building.

After completing his elective term and resigning as president, Beck is carried from the convention hall on the shoulders of delegates. Beck resigned to devote his time to his wife, Dorothy, who unbeknownst to anyone other than Beck and one physician, had only a short time to live.

Beck's farewell address to the Teamsters convention in 1957.

We made our point; now, I hope that the Teamsters and the A.F.ofL. will get back together again someday, when there's a sense of understanding. That's important. What is not important are the egos of a Dave Beck or a George Meany or a Walter Reuther. The only thing that really matters is the welfare of the men and women who make up the membership of those international unions.

10
Fadeout

J UNE 12, 1957.

At the end of a long day, Dave Beck flipped out the lights as he walked out of his office at union headquarters in Seattle. He always turned out the lights, to save money. He was thinking about a late dinner. Then he remembered his diet. Oh, the hell with his weight. On this evening he would eat a big meal and be good to himself. He had always believed in the good life. "What is good enough for General Motors is good enough for Dave Beck," he told himself expansively.

But he was already thinking about a more conservative lifestyle. On May 26, he had formally announced that he would not run for re-election as general president of Teamsters International. This provoked a mad scramble for his job. Jimmy Hoffa would be a candidate; so would Einar Mohn; so would Harold Gibbons, the St. Louis Teamsters' official, who once said: "The hell with Congress, we're building a union!"

139

As he walked out of his office this night, Beck at age 63 was complacent. The feet that carried him across the sidewalk were clad in socks bearing the initials DB. At the curb stood his air-conditioned Cadillac. The left hand that helped support him as he stepped into the car glistened with a three-diamond ring that the Elks Lodge #92 gave as a parting gift when he finished his year as Exalted Ruler in 1929. And he still had a rent-free ranch-type mansion, with a pool and artificial waterfall. He was not yet a millionaire, but he was well on his way to being one. When he retired in September, he would receive from the Teamsters a lifetime pension of $50,000 a year.

And he still had some very good friends. Sure, some ingrates had deserted him, but there were still some genuine friends; friends who would say stoutly, as one did: "What the hell did Dave do that was so wrong? Look at what the Teamsters got out of it. They have higher pay and better working conditions than they ever had under Dan Tobin." Beck, himself, could go along with that. "Who the hell should I apologize to?" he asked reporters. "I let my conscience be my guide!" He said he slept the sleep of the just and innocent. "I go to bed at night and I never wake up until morning," he said. "I've been in this for 40 years and whatever happens doesn't bother me."

Despite his national prominence, Beck's heart remained in Seattle. "I would rather be a lamppost on Seattle's Second Avenue," he often said, "than own all of Miami Beach."

In Seattle, Beck was king. He lived in one of the nation's most remarkable neighborhood complexes. His own place included broad lawns, elaborate rock gardening, an artificial waterfall, and a junior-sized railroad for the entertainment of the neighborhood kids. Beck could even take a refreshing dip in his tiled, heated swimming pool. On hand to escort him, and to rub him down afterward, were some of "The Boys" from "Chez Beck," the compound facing Lake Washington. When it was built, also thrown up around it was a cluster of relatively modest homes to be occupied by relatives and close associates. They included:

Norman Gessert, a cousin of Beck's wife. Another resident of the Compound was Richard Klinge, former University of Washington football guard and classmate of Beck Jr. Klinge was one of Papa Beck's early-morning walking companions, served as his masseur, and was secretary-treasurer of a Teamster local. Then there was Albert Irvine; Jack Stackpool, another former Washington football star (fullback), who alternated with Klinge as Beck's hiking pal, also a business agent for a Teamster local; Mrs. Lemuel Beck, Dave's 87-year-old mother, and Dave's sister, Mrs. Reta Henne, a switchboard operator at the Teamsters headquarters in Seattle; and Joe McEvoy, husband of Beck's niece.

"I've been as goddamn interested in all these kids as I have been in my own son," Beck said in 1957. "That's why I developed the lakefront compound and sold their places to them at cost, loaning them the money where it was necessary."

For Dave Beck, there was no place like Seattle. From the windows of his office he could point out across Taylor Avenue to five lots that he owned. Around the corner on Denny Way was the service station he co-owned with Frank Brewster, chairman of the Western Conference of Teamsters. Nearby were the two parking lots Beck bought for $28,000 after pleading with the Teamsters to buy them first. Looming over the entire area was the Grosvenor House apartment-hotel that Beck and friends built in 1949.

"Real estate is my dish," Beck said at the time. "Recently I've cashed in at least $900,000 in real-estate holdings. Sure, I've made money. But that's also part of the way I have increased the assets of the international union by $9 million since I became president."

In his private life, Beck often spent a quiet evening with his wife Dorothy, a gentle, grey-haired woman who suffered from high blood pressure and asthma.

Beck loved to read. "I've read nearly everything ever written about Napoleon," he said in 1957. "I just got through *Citadel* by William White of the *New York Times*, and incidentally, it's a hell of a condemnation of the excesses in congressional investigations."

He also enjoyed television. He doted on big-money quiz shows. "I do fairly good on some of those questions," he said. One of Dave's friends, in an analytic mood, said that "when Dave talks about money, it's like some other guy talking about a beautiful woman—he gets a gleam in his eye. The only pinup in Beck's mind is that good green stuff with numbers on it."

Some nights Beck dressed in slacks and pocket-monogrammed smoking jacket to play host in the underground layout that was the real showplace of his home. Some of the Compound's boys were always on hand to run the 35-mm. CinemaScope movie projectors in his 45-seat theater. Others were ready to tend the bar, embellished with a union label and well-stocked both in booze and in soft drinks for Beck, the teetotaler. Also on the underground level was a ballroom, complete with blond electric organ, a spinet piano, and a carefully illuminated portrait of President Beck. On occasion, Dave would take a visitor out back and point out the apartment above his four-car garage, where the Compound's rotating bodyguards lived. The bodyguards were constantly on hand because Beck was positive that an unknown "they" were looking for a chance to kidnap his son, a powerful 35-year-old, 210-pounder.

The closer Beck got to retirement, the more the idea appealed to him. "Hell," he revealed to a reporter, "nothing I've done in the whole world has made Mrs. Beck any happier than when I told her I was quitting. Go ahead, go ahead and ask her." The reporter did, but before Dorothy Beck could answer, Dave was excitedly egging her on. "Go ahead," he cried. "Go ahead, tell him how happy it's made you!"

But in actual fact, if it hadn't been for Mrs. Beck's illness, Beck probably would have had to be carried out of the presidency feet first and kicking furiously. Shortly before he learned that his wife was dying, he gave every indication that he would serve another five-year term. "Why am I staying?" he asked an interviewer. "Why will I run for re-election next September—and win? I'm staying because I love the labor movement. Why does a Catholic priest stay on? Why a minister? Why scientists? Why professors? That's their life. The Teamsters are my life. I don't think they have paid me a goddamn cent more than I've been worth, and any day they can get another man, let them go get him."

Then Dave got the tragic news from his wife's doctor—asthma and bad heart, five years to live—and all that changed. "I owe her," Dave said. "I owe her those five years."

As Dave Beck made plans to retire to be with his wife, a guessing game was building up as to his successor. Would it be the uncommunicative Mohn? Harold Gibbons? Maybe Bill Lee of Chicago? What about Jimmy Hoffa, the fast-rising boss of the Teamsters Central States Conference? Though Hoffa had often been the target for accusations he had never been stuck with a major scandal. Jimmy had a police record "maybe as long as your arm," but he emerged triumphant from an earlier congressional investigation and was a big favorite to win the election.

Brewster? Forget him. He wasn't running. Newspaper headlines had tarnished his public image. Details of the story hit the fan when James Elkins, a 56-year-old racketeer in Portland, testified at the McClellan committee hearings that he had secretly made tapes (with a hidden recorder inside his coat) linking a local district attorney, a sheriff, and 33 others with crime in the city. Both the district attorney and sheriff were indicted by a grand jury for taking bribes. They had won their jobs with backing from Western Teamsters. Bobby Kennedy hammered away at Elkins, trying to draw a connection between the Teamsters and a takeover of the rackets in Portland.

Jim Elkins, who dealt mainly in gambling and bootlegging, was by far the most articulate member of the cast of witnesses called by Kennedy. While others ducked behind the Fifth Amendment, Elkins talked. At one point, Kennedy asked him if he had ever had any previous brushes with the law in Oregon.

"Yes," Elkins said. "Once I went to pick up two slot machines and got shot when I was putting them in my car."

"What happened?" Kennedy asked.

"Well," Elkins told the Senate committee, "there were several people standing there on the porch watching us and one of them hollered at me something that attracted my attention and I looked around and he was hitting at me with a gun, and I turned around and hit him. He was bootlegging, too, and he had a 15-year-old boy with an old rusty Luger pointing at me. He started shooting about that time and shot me through the side. I am telling the boy who is driving the car, 'Let's get away from here,' and he said, 'He has that thing pointed at me,' and I said, 'It is darn funny. He is pointing at you and he is hitting *me*.'"

Elkins also said that once in Arizona, in 1931, he got 20 to 30 years for assault with intent to kill.

"You had been in partnership with a policeman at that time, is that right?" Kennedy asked.

"Well," Elkins replied, "let's just say I was cutting a little money."

"And then you had a plan with the policeman to move into a place, and as you came in he started to shoot you, is that right?"

"Well, I believe he was going to shoot the boy that was with me, but I shot back."

"Did you hit him?"

"Not bad, no."

"And then, in 1938, you got 15 months in San Francisco for possession of narcotics. Right?"

"And you served your year then. A year and a day."

"That is correct."

"I did, yes, sir. I picked up a package at the American Express office for a friend."

"Then did you have any difficulty after that?"

"Not after that."

Once his own shady past was spread upon the record, Elkins proceeded with the same candor and detail to testify as to the activities of the union in Portland—a story that was to prove very embarrassing to a mixed passel of regional Teamsters and Oregon politicians.

According to Elkins' testimony, the Teamsters' invasion of Portland's rackets was undertaken by Tom Maloney, allegedly representing Teamster headquarters in Seattle. Elkins told the Senate committee that Maloney first fixed things up, for a price, so that Elkins' pinball machines would be given union stickers.

"Once this was done," Elkins said, "Portland Teamsters were persuaded by their officials to support Bill Langley in his campaign for district attorney. Langley formerly was a partner of mine. Once he was elected, both the gamblers and the Teamsters had a friend at court."

Maloney and his friends then started to cut the Portland operators out entirely and Elkins said he tried to persuade Brewster to "call that gorilla back to Seattle and back into his cage."

As the hearings wound down in front of the Senate rackets committee, Jimmy Hoffa could afford to smile. He had come out of the rackets investigations with a clean bill of health. Labor experts and professional handicappers were already picking him as a shoo-in when the Teamsters got ready to elect their next president.

11
Time
of Trial

THE years 1957-1964 were a low period in the life of Dave Beck. And he had to face them with the whole world looking on.

First, there was his wife Dorothy's fatal illness. Dr. Alexander Grinstein prophetically told Beck that she had only five more years to live (he missed by just two months), and Beck spent much of his time devoted to her. The rest of his attention focused on his growing legal battles.

The axe first fell on March 12, 1957, in the form of a 445-page report turned in by federal investigator Claude J. Watson and some 50 agents who assisted him. Later, when grand jury hearings broke up in Seattle and Tacoma, Beck faced indictments charging him with (1) "assisting with the filing of a fradulent 1950 tax return for the Joint Council No. 28 Building Association," and (2) allegedly "selling a 1952 Cadillac belonging to the Teamsters and pocketing the $1,900."

The federal government also tried to get a conviction involving $240,000 in back income taxes for the years 1950-

1953, but the U.S. Circuit Court of Appeals in San Francisco and Judge George H. Boldt in Federal District Court in Tacoma, in separate hearings, ruled in favor of Beck and dismissed the government's claims.

In the case of the Cadillac, Beck steadfastly denied taking the money received from the sale of the union-owned automobile, pointing out that it was turned in to the Seattle Teamster office and track of it lost through involved bookkeeping procedures. His conviction of grand larceny eventually went on to the State Supreme Court in Olympia, where, in a rare 4 to 4 decision, it was upheld. Judge Harry E. Foster disqualified himself. He once served as an attorney for the Teamsters Union. With the high court evenly split, the King County Superior Court ruling stood.

Beck told reporters that he had been confident of a reversal on the grounds he had not received a fair trial in his home county. "Apparently four of the judges felt the same way," Beck said at the time. Much of his appeal from the grand larceny conviction was based on his assertion of misconduct and bias in the grand jury proceedings leading to the Superior Court trial. Beck said that some members of the grand jury were prejudiced against him. He also maintained that the King County Superior Court should have granted him a copy of the grand jury proceedings.

"State charges that I pocketed the $1,900 were far-fetched," Beck said. "These are the facts: Guiry Marcella was my secretary in our Seattle office and she received a sales payment for the Cadillac, belonging to the Teamsters, which I had been using whenever I was in the Northwest. She promptly deposited the check in the International account. When she advised me of her action, I corrected her immediately. 'No, no, no,' I told her over the telephone from Washington. 'That's not where it goes.' So she changed it, but instead of holding the check until I got back to Seattle and putting it in the right account, she deposited it in my own *personal* account. As soon as I found out about her second error, I quickly reimbursed the union for the $1,900. That was the legal issue right there. Obviously, the grand jury didn't believe my version of what really happened. In any event, they charged me with grand larceny and the indictment stuck. Guilty? Hell, no."

The conviction carried a sentence up to 15 years in prison. Under Washington law, that was mandatory. Superior Court Judge George H. Revelle and Prosecutor Charles O. Carroll both recommended that Beck serve only three years. Beck received the sentence without any show of emotion. Staring out the sunlit courtroom window for a moment after Judge Revelle finished speaking, he coughed softly and turned away. Dave Beck could take it as well as dish it out.

The federal indictment was more complicated. Officially, it stated: "That on or about the 15th of May, 1952, in the Southern Division of the Western District of Washington, David D. Beck, also known as Dave Beck, did wilfully and knowingly aid and assist in, and counsel, procure and advise the preparation and presentation to the Collector of Internal Revenue for the Internal Revenue Collection District of Washington, at Tacoma, Washington, of a false and fraudulent United States Annual Return of Organization. Exempt from Income Tax Form 990, of Joint Council #28, Building Association, for the calendar year 1950, in which said return it was represented that the said Joint Council #28, Building Association, had expended moneys in the amount of $16,718.17, for building payments and alterations, in the category or miscellaneous expenses attributable to income from rents, the said defendant then and there well knew that Joint Council #28, Building Association, had not expended moneys in the amount of $16,718.17 for building payments and alterations, in the category of miscellaneous expenses attributable to income from rent, but had in truth and in fact expended a substantially lesser sum."

Judge George Boldt in Tacoma found the defendant guilty, and the decision was upheld by a higher court after a long series of legal maneuvers by Beck's attorneys.

After years of silence, Beck recently gave his version of the events leading up to his conviction.

"When our Annual Report of Joint Council #28 was sent to the Internal Revenue Service, my signature was not on it," Beck recounted. "As head of the Joint Council in 1950, my name was supposed to be on it, but it wasn't for a very logical reason. *I never even saw the report.* My secretary said she never saw it, either. So put it down as a bookkeeping blooper—and a costly one for me. Somehow, I don't know how, but it turned up in Washington, D.C. unsigned by me. According to testimony at the trial in Tacoma, that Annual Report was put on my desk in Seattle. Legally, technically, as head of the Joint Council at the time, I was held responsible for seeing to it that the report was properly filed and signed. It wasn't. So when the federal government went after me in 1957 and charged me with sending in a 'fraudulent United States Annual Return of Organization,' I took the blame. It went with the job. I have often wondered, though, why it took the government so long to make an issue out of it. That was in 1950—and they never sought an indictment until 1957!"

Beck was sentenced to five years. Both the Federal Parole Board and the Washington State Parole Board agreed to let him serve his federal and state sentences at McNeil Island concurrently and set his minimum term at two years. The state board said he would probably be paroled simultaneously with his release from McNeil.

Beck:

"Even now, 20 years after the trials, newspaper and magazine writers still make the mistake of saying I went to prison on income tax *evasion* charges. I wish they would get the facts straight," Beck has said several times. "Each time this is brought to my attention, either I or my attorneys contact the publications in question and ask them if they want to invite a libel suit. I am very sensitive about that error, because I was never convicted of any personal income tax evasion, and when the papers make such a statement I ask for an immediate retraction and always get it. Seven or eight times in recent years, newspapers have had to run retractions for falsely reporting in their articles that "Dave Beck went to prison for evasion of income taxes." I might add that I have never lost a libel suit. Down the years I have filed four of them and have yet to lose. Every one of the suits was settled out of court, too, because the defendants surely didn't want to go to court and be proved wrong. So let's put the question of evasion of personal income taxes to rest once and for all. It just isn't a part of my record. *I have never been convicted of evasion of taxes."*

One positive note that came out of the two-and-a-half years of the McClellan committee hearings was the Landrum-Griffin Bill. It was made into law in 1959 and modified the Taft-Hartley Act. The Landrum-Griffin Bill imposed restrictions on the management of unions; specifically, the manner in which union leaders filed their reports with the Secretary of Labor.

12
Life on
an Island

"There are two places where you'll find your real *self*
—war and in prison. I've experienced both."

Egyptian President Anwar Sadat, 1978

ON the morning of June 20, 1962, a front as
dank as an Olympia oyster moved up the bay. The smell of
showers was in the air. Dave Beck stepped out of a pale
gray car with the letters "Deputy U.S. Marshal" on the
sides. With him were two attorneys, Charles Burdell and
James McMahon. Dapper and smiling, Beck was dressed
expensively in a gray suit, gray hat, and he wore dark sunglasses. The point of a white handkerchief protruded from
his breastpocket.

Outwardly, Beck had not lost any of his customary
self-confidence. If you hadn't read the morning papers, you
would not have guessed he was on his way to begin serving a
five-year hitch in the Federal penitentiary at McNeil
Island, a 20-minute boat ride from mainland Tacoma.
Leading up to this hour, the Associated Press reviewed the
Beck story in detail:

Dave Beck fought his way up in the brawling, bare-knuckle, head-knocking days of labor organizing on the West Coast to the top of the International Teamsters Union, the nation's largest. He wielded tremendous power. In his climb from laundry truck driver he amassed a fortune and is a reputed millionaire.

But trouble suddenly descended on this man who had achieved success also in business and became a civic leader. Late in 1957 he was convicted in Seattle Superior Court of grand larceny. The specific charge was the theft of $1,900 from the sale of a union-owned Cadillac.

Beck was sentenced to up to five years' imprisonment. (The state board of prison terms and paroles fixes the actual time to be served.) The conviction was appealed.

"Beck's union powers were broad," said a defense lawyer, "but he had no authority to take union money. So, if he did use that money, it would have to constitute a *loan*, and money received from the union as loans is not taxable. He has repaid $370,000."

Any tax mistakes made by Beck, the defense argued, were the result of ignorance as he left the filing of returns to others. Beck did not testify in his defense. U.S. District Judge George H. Boldt sentenced Beck to five years in prison and fined him $60,000 on the income tax conviction. An appeal was announced.

In sentencing Beck, Judge Boldt gave him a harsh lecture: "Exposure of your insatiable greed, resulting in your fall from high place, is a sad and shocking story. You have plundered your union, your intimate associates, and in some instances your personal friends, most of whom quite readily would have given you anything you asked. You have cheated every last humble American who pays income taxes by attempting to evade your personal taxes and thus cast your share of the tax burden on your fellow citizens—the vast majority of whom are infinitely less able to bear tax burdens than you."

Afterwards, Beck told reporters: "I am not the first innocent person to be sentenced, nor will I be the last. I'll comment on Judge Boldt's remarks later."

Beck lost an appeal to have his sentence reduced.

Judge Boldt said he felt the sentence was fair, both to Beck and the public. "It is entirely appropriate to his serious and extensive criminal offenses," the judge said. "This was stated and explained directly to him when I pronounced sentence in open court. Nothing whatever, coming to my attention since that time, shows or even intimates misjudgment in the penalty originally imposed or presents a basis for its modification in any particular. This conclusion is fully supported by the appellate ruling in the case, both in language and result. To my knowledge, Mr. Beck has never publicly expressed or indicated acknowledgment of or regret for his grievous wrong-doing. He has not been exonerated from any criminal offense charged in this case, and is not now in prison to account for merely technical crimes. Any intimation to the contrary would be false and grossly deceptive."

Under normal parole procedures, Beck would serve a minimum of 20 months. In his petition, he asked that he (1) be allowed to become eligible for parole at such time as the board of parole determined; (2) that the sentence imposed have a one-year term designated after which he would be eligible for parole; (3) that the sentence be reduced to a term of four years and 11 months on each count, to run concurrently; or (5), that his commitment be made the subject of a study to be conducted by the director of the Bureau of Prisons, James V. Bennett, and that subsequent action of the court be based on this study.

As Beck approached the prison boat waiting to take him to McNeil Island, approximately 50 members of the press stood assembled at the dock; representatives of all the principal Washington papers, the major wire services, photographers, and TV cameramen. Beck knew most of them by their first names. One reporter, Dick Monagham, of the *Tacoma News Tribune*, had already filed his advance for the early afternoon edition: "Dave Beck Starts Life Behind Bars."

The AP man asked in a soft voice, "Are you nervous, Dave?"

Beck shook his head. "Not at all," he said.

"Any regrets?"

"Yes," he said, suddenly turning serious. "This whole procedure has brought great sorrow to my 93-year-old mother, my sister and her family, and to my son. I am just happy that my wife, God bless her soul, is not here to see this."

Dorothy Beck, his wife of 43 years, had succumbed to asthma and a heart condition the previous November.

Reminded of Judge Boldt's harsh words when he sentenced him, Beck told the press corps that it was the duty of every American citizen to accept the final verdicts of the courts. "And I do so now in that spirit," Beck said. "But I assure my family and friends that I have never knowingly violated income tax rules or any other law. I have never broken my word. I never will."

A brief silence followed this recital. Then with a crisp salute, Beck said, "What was it General MacArthur said at Corregidor? 'I'll be back.' Well, that goes for me, too. You don't have to fall down just because you've been knocked down. What matters is, do you get up again?"

Beck shook hands all around, then turned himself over to Deputy U.S. Marshal Dick Osborn, and was gone.

From a distance, the great cream-colored walls of McNeil stood out like a giant fortress, bleak, oppressive, impregnable. Few prisoners had ever escaped from there. It is the oldest federal penitentiary in America. Behind those steep walls are the usual cement streets and barren cell blocks and workshops. The prison population averaged about 1,100; their crimes ranged from sophisticated bank robberies to stock fraud to cannibalism. Cannibalism? One of the prisoners, an Eskimo, was serving life for *eating his wife*. Fortunately, he had no complaints about the prison food.

Once a year, the editors of the *Island Lantern* magazine, a prison publication produced by the inmates themselves, came out with a calendar. The calendar was unique in that it highlighted dates of especial interest to its "captured" audience. Sample:

Jan. 12, Ruth Snyder becomes first woman to be electrocuted, 1928.

Feb. 3, Belle Starr dies, 1889; Feb. 14, St. Valentine's Day massacre, Chicago, 1929.

April 1, National Con Artists Day; April 14, J.W. Booth shoots Abraham Lincoln, 1865.

May 3, Clyde Barrow and Bonnie Parker killed, 1933.

July 25, 'Custer's mistake,' 1876; July 22, John Dillinger killed, 1934.

Sprinkled throughout the calendar were appropriate quotes. Such as this from that thoughtful philosopher, Al Capone: "You can get much farther with a kind word and a gun than you can with a kind word alone." And this from Jerome K. Jerome: "It is always the best policy to speak the truth; unless, of course, you are an exceptionally good liar."

There were also some illustrations, such as a photo of a cell door in McNeil's first cellblock, built in 1875, with the caption: "The cells were 4 by 7 feet and furnished with straw mats and two buckets—one for drinking water." And there was a drawing of a big, black 1930 Chrysler, with some advertising copy: "When choosing your 'Getaway Car,' much time and consideration has to be taken to insure the maximum in efficiency and standard features. Compare and experience for yourself the ease of exchanging machine-gun fire from the enormous windows—eight in all—and note the spacious running boards, able to support three hit men on each side. The doors make this the first auto ever to insure easy entry when the G-men return fire. And don't overlook the V-12 engine capable of breezing you out of that tight spot and taking you luxuriously to the next town, swiftly and economically. Yes, Chrysler sets a new standard which the modern gangster cannot fail to acclaim."

Oh, McNeil Island was going to be one big barrel of laughs. Sure.

Beck relates his experiences:

Hey, it wasn't so bad. I had few complaints. A federal prison certainly beats a state pen. And, hell, the food, comfort, and conveniences sure surpassed the way we lived in World War I. Besides, I had mentally prepared myself for McNeil. I knew I wasn't over there for a picnic. I was there to do time. It was just a matter of adjustment.

On the positive side, I lost weight in prison, something my personal physician was always nagging me to do. From the time I entered McNeil, I vowed I'd slim down. That was the biggest plus of even being in prison. So I jogged a lot on the cinder track they had; practically every day, weather permitting. I was 67 years old, too, but I never felt it. There were those who wondered if I'd even survive McNeil. I never entertained such negative thoughts. I *knew* I'd make it, and no favors asked. I was full of spunk and determination and had an instinct for self-preservation. If you want to know the truth, I was damn curious about life in a prison. I had heard so many conflicting stories. Now, by damn, I could see for myself.

People have since asked me to compare federal penitentiaries. The only one I know anything about is McNeil. Yet, this is an actual fact: When Alcatraz was eliminated, a great number of its inmates were shipped to McNeil. Frankie Carbo, the notorious mobster who had links with the fight racket for years, was among the transfers. I heard Frankie and maybe 30 other guys say they'd rather do time at Alcatraz. They preferred the isolation, felt McNeil was "too close to the mainland." On "the rock," they could mind their own business and take every day as it came. Nobody was giving them any special attention, and that was preferential to McNeil, where there were a lot of visitors.

Being in prison, I couldn't help but reflect sometimes

why I was there. You can toss out what Judge Boldt said about me. His assessment of me was too extreme. But I wasn't going to argue with him. No, my conclusions were that I was simply the victim of the work I had been doing; caught up in the efforts of the political opposition to labor; to go after the leadership and destroy it if they could. Technically, that's where I wound up, too, but I wasn't going to let it destroy me.

I want to state right now—and I ask you to go back and read Judge Boldt's vicious summation of me when he passed sentence—when he was reversed one-hundred percent by a higher court, he did not retract one word of his diatribe—nor has he to this day!

I also had lots of time to think about religion; I mean, my personal commitment to God. Sure, I believe in God. I was born a Catholic. My mother was a Catholic, my father was not. He converted to Catholicism when he married mother. Early in my own life, I took the position that, regardless of anything else, whenever I married, I'd marry into the religion of my wife. Where children are involved, I always have felt that the mother should be closer to them than the father, so it is important that she choose the faith. I followed that rule in both of my marriages. My first wife was Presbyterian. When she died and I married a second time, my second wife was Episcopalian. I feel close to both churches.

I think I was a good husband, a good father. With clear conscience, I can say I was always faithful to both my wives. Absolutely. There was never any hanky-panky. In any problem that I was faced with—in which morality was involved—I'd ask myself, "Well, what is mother going to think?" I never forced my moral ethics on anyone else. We must all live our own lives.

McCallum:

There was no one to greet Beck when he got off the prison boat at McNeil. He did not have to be a genius to figure out that there was a "message" in the fact. Nobody was going to give him preferential treatment. "I was just another number," he told me recently.

For the first few weeks, Beck was put in "Admission and Orientation," or "fish tank." As a newcomer, he was stripped, showered, given a close neck trim and supplied with a coarse denim uniform and work shoes. Then he was sent to the prison hospital for a full physical examination. After all that, he was interviewed by a caseworker, whose object was to try to determine what sort of person he was and how he would adjust to prison life. "I later heard that Warden Paul J. Madigan, formerly the warden at Alcatraz, figured I was probably a farmhand type," Beck remembered. "At McNeil, you either serve your time inside the main institution or out on the farm. The difference is that on the farm you live in a dormitory and work among the 50 acres of vegetables, 130 acres of fruit trees, the dairy herd, or the hogs. The farm makes the island nearly self-sustaining. Most prisoners prefer the farm to the cellhouses."

Beck's status was up to the Classification Committee, which was composed of Warden Madigan, two associate wardens, the caseworkers, the educational supervisor, a medical specialist, and others. His financial status as a prisoner was a come-down from his practices as a millionaire businessman with a $160,000 home. Prison rules allowed him only $15 a month for such commissary purchases as toilet articles, candy, or ice cream. He wasn't permitted any walking-around money, however. The $15 he spent at the commissary was deducted from the balance he had on deposit.

While Beck was in the Admission and Orientation section, he had to get up each day at 6:30 a.m. and be in bed by 10 p.m. If he got assigned to the farm, he'd be expected to rise at 6 a.m. Television was taboo while he was still in the admission program, but it was available on the farm and in certain units within the walls.

Beck was told by his caseworker that he could subscribe to his hometown newspapers and one other, plus five or six magazines. "You will *not*, however, be allowed to run any of your many businesses from here," he was advised, "and you are permitted one visit from your family every two weeks."

After Beck finished the two weeks of orientation, Warden Madigan told newspaper reporters that he thought Dave "will adjust to prison life in good shape."

Beck:

On the whole, though, let me make it clear that I have no protest to make against the time I spent in prison. I hold no grudge against the people who sent me there. To be perfectly frank, my prison term actually added 10 years to my life. In retrospect, it was a vacation. But let's be honest, too. I didn't want to go to prison. Only a damned fool prefers such a life. Hell, no one chooses incarceration over freedom. Still, it wasn't so bad. I was prepared for the experience. I had been the eye of a hurricane in hundreds of bloody disputes in the American labor movement, and I don't know how many times my enemies tried to crucify me for the positions I took against big business. I won four or five major libel suits in those campaigns to destroy me, too. I never lost a libel suit; I always won. So because of this feisty nature of mine, there'd been built up inside of me a tough-hided capacity to accept life as it came. When I landed at McNeil, I thought to myself, *Okay, you're here, now make the best of it. This is part of the price you must pay for being a scrapper.* What was I supposed to do, cry?

I was 67 years old. I had been working 17 and 18 hours a day. For two years my wife had been dying. I finally lost her just prior to reporting to McNeil. It was thus with heavy heart that I walked into prison.

I quickly adjusted. The change of lifestyle was just what the doctor ordered. For one example, I entered into a physical fitness program. I lived regular hours. Instead of shooting back and forth all over the U.S. and even the world on labor matters—New York one week, Paris and London the next, and back to Seattle at my desk in between, working long dawn-to-dusk hours—I was in bed every night by 9 o'clock at least 28 out of every 30 days. I got at least nine hours of sleep. The dark circles under my eyes disappeared. My belly went from flab to hard muscle. I lost 30 pounds.

The only request I made of officials was that I be given an opportunity to be assigned to the farm. I felt the duty would give me a better chance to get my body in shape. I was turned down. I don't know why; maybe they were just testing me or it was probably just more politics. Eighteen months later I was told I could go to the farm, but then it was my turn to say no. I wanted no favors from them. I was working in the cannery and liked it. The job was easy. I don't mean I didn't have problems. Of course, I had them. Plenty.

Ten years before, I had suffered from a series of kidney stone attacks and several times spent time in Providence Hospital and Swedish Hospital in Seattle and another hospital down in Miami, but each time I passed the stones successfully. My personal physician always had advised me not to let anyone operate on me. "Under no circumstances," he warned me. Then at McNeil, this one day, I felt an excruciating knife-like pain shooting across the lower part of my back. I thought I was going to die then and there. Wracked by pain all night, I reported to sick call the following morning. Four or five medical assistants were in charge—not real doctors but just medical aides assigned to minor ailments.

When it came to my turn, one of the aides gazed at me skeptically. "Well," he asked, "what's your beef?"

"I want permission to talk to the chief doctor," I said.

"Permission—permission? Permission for what, for chrissake?"

"For pains in my lower back," I said.

"What's the matter with you?"

"I don't know."

"You don't know!"

"No," I said. "That's why I want to see the doctor. I'm hurting like hell. I have a recent history of kidney stones."

There were about 40 more guys waiting in line behind me. Nodding toward them, he said to me, "Can't you see we're busy as hell. The doctor's too busy to see you. Here, take these." He handed me two aspirin and waved me away.

"Aspirin," I protested. "I don't want any aspirin. I want to see the doctor."

Hands on hips, the aide faced me squarely.

"That's impossible," he said. "Didn't I make myself clear?"

I refused to budge.

"I want to see the doctor," I said, crisply. "I *insist* on my rights."

"The hell with your rights!" he shouted. "Don't try throwing your weight around in here! You're just another new number, to me."

In the old days, I probably would have leveled him right then and there. But this was a wiser, calmer Dave Beck. Controlling myself, I said softly, "I will tell you only once more: I must have the doctor examine me."

He finally went over to one of the other assistants, a fellow whose main duty seemed to be doling out various pills and medicine, and whispered something to him. Now this assistant confronted me. "What are you doing, Beck?" he said. "Creating trouble?" By this time the room had grown very silent. Everybody was listening. They knew me from seeing me on TV and on covers of magazines and newspapers.

"I wasn't creating trouble," I said. "The solution is simple. Just let me see the doctor."

"What's your problem?"

"I don't know. That's why I want to see the doctor. I know damn well *you* can't help me."

He looked at me dumbly and said, "Well, you can't see him, that's all there is to it."

"All right, forget it," I said, and I brushed straight past him and into the doctor's waiting room. I made myself at home in a chair outside his office. I must have sat there for 10 minutes, when finally the doctor appeared. He looked at me stuffily and growled, "How'd you get in here?" By now I was pretty well steamed up myself. I clenched my fists.

"The same way you got in—through the door there," I told him.

His face suddenly turned white.

"Wait a minute, mister," he said. "I'm not going to talk to you. Get outta here!"

"That's fine," I bristled. "But there's just one question I want answered: next week, in federal court, we will find out *why* you refused to talk to me. I make only one request. There are three people in this room, listening to everything we're saying. All I want from you is that you be man enough to repeat in front of a judge your refusal to give me medical service; agree to that and I'll leave."

There was a brief silence. I sensed that my little speech was effective.

"Just a moment," he said finally. He left the room and went back inside his office and dialed the phone. "Hello, John?" I couldn't hear all the talk, but there was much of it, and when he came back to me, he said, "Okay, *Mister* Beck, let's have a look at you."

I followed him into his office, took off my shirt and undershirt, and said, "I want an X-ray. I have a history of kidney stones. I know the symptoms and I've been having attacks."

The doctor waggled his finger at me to put my clothes back on. "Where are we going?" I wanted to know.

"To the hospital for that X-ray," he said.

Later, after studying the pictures, the doctor threw up his hands and declared, "Holy God, Beck, you got pneumonia. I'm putting you to bed."

"Well," I said, "I knew damn well aspirin wasn't powerful enough to kill what I have."

I spent the next two weeks in the prison hospital, and after I came out, I had no more serious trouble with the medics, though I did write a letter to a friend in Congress complaining about the hospital services at McNeil. Doctors would come over from the mainland, perform surgery on the inmates, and then leave them in the care of prison aides who lacked the training and ability to look after them. This was the basis of the letter I wrote to my congressman. Obviously, there were repercussions, because it wasn't long before I was being summoned before another doctor—the chief sawbones himself. He looked me up and down severely.

"So you're the great Dave Beck," he said. "You write letters. You write the kind of letters that get us into trouble."

If he was trying to get my goat, his sarcasm didn't work. I said, "That's right. There's nothing in the rules here that says I can't write letters, is there? I'm allowed to write letters to anyone I want—even congressmen."

He quickly dismissed me. The subject never came up again. The matter was closed.

One warden at McNeil during my imprisonment was Paul J. Madigan. The inmates were different with him somehow than they were with almost anyone else—that was a feeling. Sometimes he'd go over to the mainland to forget it all, and as he moved from place to place, one of his "graduates" would come up to him and say, "Gezchris, the warden!" and step over with his hat off and hand held out. "Warden, harya? It's good to see you again!" Almost always the warden had the man's name. They were like grown men with an old professor they had loved as undergraduates. It wasn't a fatuous admiration, it had the essence of genuine gratitude and of aboriginal trust. They could trust him because he trusted them.

One morning on my way to the cannery, Warden Madigan called me out of line. "Mr. Beck," he said, "you've never been to see me."

"No," I said, "I have never been to see you. But you never called me out of the line to tell me that. What is it you want to tell me, Mr. Madigan?"

"There are two people coming over on the 11 o'clock boat who want to talk to you."

"Who are they?"

"They're from Washington, D.C. Government men."

"What do they want?"

"Information about Jimmy Hoffa."

"Hoffa?"

He nodded.

"No disrespect, Warden, but I plain won't talk to them about Hoffa," I said. "No, no, no. If they want to talk to me about Dave Beck, fine. I'm willing to sit down and tell 'em anything they want to know about Dave Beck; subject, of course, to my right to first make a phone call to my attorney in Seattle stipulating as to what I may say. We may still have litigation pending in the courts for the next four or five years, and I must routinely protect myself."

"Yes, yes," the warden agreed. "But they only want to talk to you about Hoffa."

"Then I can't help them," I said. "I'm not going to discuss or answer any questions about Hoffa. No, nothing doing."

The warden was a sly old dog.

"Well, it might be to your advantage, within a reasonable period of time, if you'd see them," He let that sink in, then, "Think about it, Mr. Beck." His words were tinged with promise. Interpretation: cooperate with federal officials and I could expect a break from the parole board. I stuck to my guns, however. "I'm still not interested," I told the warden. "Well," he said, "suit yourself. If you change your mind, come see me."

Though he was a good guy and I had a high regard for him, I never spoke to the warden again.

McCallum:

Dave Beck first met Jimmy Hoffa in 1936. Their association was mostly business. They seldom saw each other socially. In 1952, after Beck was made president of the Teamsters, Hoffa was elected a vice-president, saying, "Everybody fears the Teamsters." He said it with pride. No one denied that a good part of this fear was due to Hoffa himself. Hoffa was many things to many people, but he was one thing to all alike: He was *tough*. A tough friend and a tough enemy; tough mentally and tough physically. Only 5'-5" in height, Hoffas was a hard 180 pounds, and he grew up in Detroit when the auto capital was one of the toughest labor towns in the nation. Hoffa once recalled, "I was hit so many times with night sticks, clubs, and brass knuckles I can't even remember where the bruises were, but I can hit back and I did. Guys who tried to break me up got broken up."

Beck:

The school in which Jimmy grew up taught him no lesson except to be tougher than the next guy. But I got along with him all right. As our friendship grew, I saw that he had a helluva lot of organizational ability, and yet he did not impress me as future presidential material for the Teamsters. No, I did not see that in him at all. A front-line troubleshooter, yes, but not president. A short time before I voluntarily stepped down as president of the Teamsters, Hoffa came to me and said, "Now, Dave, if you are going to run again, I will not be a candidate." I told him, "Hell, Jimmy, I don't know what I'm going to do myself." But I *did* know. Sure, I knew, because the doctors had already confided in me that my wife, Dorothy, was dying. At most, she would live for only six or seven more years, and I owed them to Dorothy. I didn't tell anybody about my decision then, because it would have placed me in a poor administrative position. Hell, if word had leaked out I was quitting to be with my sick wife, all of the Teamster officers would have been scurrying around building political fences, so I waited until four months before I left office to make the announcement. Prior to the press conference, I called Hoffa, Jack Gannon, and several others out to a beach place I was staying at in Santa Monica and told them of my decision not to run for another term.

In the ensuing race to fill my shoes, Hoffa won easily. I had changed my earlier convictions about him. Totally dedicated to the labor movement, a man of great self-discipline, when there was work to be done, he did it, even if it meant a 24-hour day. He hardly knew what it was to relax. I liked that. I also liked the fact that he neither smoked nor drank nor partied around. He took his wife along to labor conventions if he could and if he couldn't, he confined himself to the convention hall and his hotel room. He was a family man and was deeply devoted to his son and daughter. His own father, a coal driller in the mines of Illinois, Kentucky, and Indiana, had died when Hoffa was only seven. Jimmy told me that he was the third of four children, and he began to earn money for the family just as soon as he was big enough. I could identify with him because I had the same experience. We were so poor my mother worked long hours in a Seattle laundry. Yes, Jimmy Hoffa and Dave Beck shared more in common than the presidency of the Teamsters.

McCallum:

On August 14, 1963, the *Tacoma News Tribune* splashed this headline across its front page: McNEIL MUM ON BECK DISCIPLINARY REPORT. There was plenty of spunk in the old boy yet! Reported the newspaper: "McNeil Island Penitentiary officials declined to comment today on an unconfirmed report that Dave Beck recently spent time in solitary confinement for a prison infraction, but they did admit Beck had been in some type of trouble. The unconfirmed report claims that the former head of the International Teamsters Union spent 10 days in 'the hole' for some sort of prison infraction.

"Today, Robert Moseley, the acting warden, filling in for Paul Madigan who has been on leave since May 13, confessed: 'Mr. Beck was in a little trouble a week or two ago, but it wasn't anything so awful.' He would not elaborate."

Coincidentally, I was sitting in the office of James V. Bennett, director of the Bureau of Prisons in Washington, D.C., when the news broke. We had been discussing the possibility of writing a book together based on his 37 years in penology. Then I asked him about Beck.

"How's he getting along at McNeil?" I wanted to know. "I've been hearing rumors. They say he's been doing some hard time."

"I'm in touch with McNeil," Bennett said. "I would say that solitary confinement is a bit exaggerated. Solitary confinement is very seldom used except in very serious offenses. We often use the term 'the hole' loosely. Sometimes it's used in referring to administrative separation—quarters away from the other prisoners—which is quite different from solitary confinement."

"Well," I said, "if Beck has broken some rule—if he has been in solitary—what effect will it have on his minimum term."

"I don't know," he said. "Certainly it won't help him."

Beck:

This is the way that was. "The Hole" is actually a prison inside a prison. It is the place to which difficult prisoners, the "hardrock" troublemakers, are now and then banished. The cells are identical. They measure only about 4' x 7' and are unfurnished except for a toilet, a basin, and a chair. At night, a guard marches you out to this pile of mattresses, and you lug one back to your cell and plop it on the bare floor. That and several army blankets constitute your bed for the night. The cell windows are very narrow and not only barred but covered wtih a wire mesh black as tar. Thus the faces of those banished to "The Hole" can be but hazily discerned by passers-by.

Outwardly, I must have appeared to the prison staff and other inmates not at all troubled by my incarceration. During my free hours, when I wasn't socializing or out on the foot track jogging, I was up in the library reading the papers, news magazines, or books. I kept up with the national labor news through *Time* and *Newsweek*. I devoured everything I could get my hands on pertaining to labor. I didn't write a lot of letters, not because there were restrictions but because of pride. I mean, I didn't want to share that low period of my life with family and friends. I never even let my mother come to see me; not even my sister. Both of them begged to come, but I wouldn't let them. They were too emotional. Seeing me in those drab prison clothes—after knowing the good life I had had all those years—would have been too painful for them. I never saw my mother again. She died before I got out of McNeil. She was 94.

One of my few regular visitors was my attorney, Eli Dorsey. He made an appointment with me one afternoon to review my late wife's estate. The meeting involved highly complex tax matters. The IRS had levied a federal income tax claim of $1.4 million against the estate. A big court battle was brewing. I was in a quandary. The prison had a rule that inmates were not supposed to run any outside business from McNeil. We could discuss just about anything else with visitors, just as long as it did not involve business. Prison officials insisted that we clear everything with our caseworker first before seeing any visitors. Well, my caseworker had about five assistants under him, and on this day he was not in his office when I dropped by to get his approval to talk to Eli Dorsey about my wife's estate. He had never censored me before, so I took my business papers into the reception room where Eli was waiting.

At first, the supervising guard paid no attention to us. He probably assumed I'd been cleared by my caseworker; I don't know. In any event, we were about 15 minutes into our meeting when I suddenly sensed that the guard was peering over my shoulder. "What do we have here, *Mister* Beck?" he asked, snatching the outline I'd been talking from. "Where's your caseworker's signature?" With that, he disappeared. Mind you, he didn't break up our meeting, he just grabbed the outline and left. It all happened so quickly, I don't think Eli was even aware of the big trouble I was in. We went ahead and finished our meeting, and he returned to the mainland on the next boat.

Several hours afterward, I was summoned before an officer and advised that I had violated prison policy. "You know what that means, Beck," he said. The penalty was banishment to "The Hole." While I made no protest, it did occur to me that the punishment was pretty stiff. But, hell, it didn't bother me, not a damn bit. I could take it. They marched me between these two big guards and stuffed me into this tiny, kennel-like concrete cell and left me there. It was dark as hell. You could have cut the silence with a knife, it was so thick. The cell was no bigger than my thumb. It had a toilet, as I said before, and a chair, nothing else. At 7 p.m. a guard appeared and marched me to this pile of mattresses, motioned for me to pick one up, and then marched me back to my cell again. Then he locked me up for the night. That's all the bed I had: a hard mattress and a couple of army blankets. Once every hour the guard popped by and squinted through the peephole, checking up on me. I curled up and dozed off.

McCallum:

Beck had no positive idea how long he'd be kept there. After a while, it seemed to him as though he existed deep underground, soundless except for snores, coughs, and the steady clack, clack, clack of the guard's hard leather heels against the cement floor. But the important thing was to keep his head. He had heard stories about "The Hole." "Sometimes," a veteran of solitary confinement said, "they throw you down there and it makes you fighting mad and crazy to boot. You curse and scream the whole time. It's intolerable." Maybe so. But it never bothered Beck a whole lot. Such an experience provokes different symptoms in different men. Claustrophobia drives some people right up the wall. The only discomfort Beck felt came from sore, stiff muscles all cramped up like that.

Beck:

People have since asked me how I kept from going off the beam cooped up down there. Well, all my life I was a fighter, tied up with labor's militant group. I had to muscle my way to the top. Nothing was ever handed to me on a silver platter. Adversity was the name of the game. It was driven into my bones. I didn't have a dime when I started. Everything I ever achieved I got myself. So I went down into "The Hole" the same way I'd gone into a thousand labor disputes—and some of those battles were big ones, too, involving the whole country. I went into "The Hole" knowing full well it couldn't break me. Hell, I'd been in situations a thousand times worse. Try fronting for a union with 1,500,000 members sometime, with 10,000 guys crying all at once for higher pay, better working conditions, relief from hunger. Hell, my phone rang off the hook 18 hours a day—"Dave do this, Dave do that." So I made up my mind I wasn't going to let solitary confinement beat me. It was like the day when I got on the boat to go to McNeil. I vowed to make it as easy as possible on myself. I remember turning to the newspaper reporters on the Steilacoom dock, just before getting on the boat, and saying "I'll return," just like General MacArthur had said. I heard through the grapevine later that Bobby Kennedy was mad as a hornet at me for my choice of words when he read about it in the *Washington Post*.

The hell with Bobby Kennedy! I paid no attention to him. I probably underrated him. *Time* once described him as "A lawyer with a true prosecutor's instinct for the jugular." *My* jugular. He publicly vowed to nail me to the cross, if not all the bosses of the Teamsters. He was full of tricks.

I have never made any secret of the fact that I disliked Bobby Kennedy intensely. It was well justified. When he was attorney general and I was at McNeil, I know damn well he sat back in Washington, D.C. pulling the strings on me. Of course, he did. I won't tell you how I know, but he was. I had people in the highest echelon at McNeil admit to me their orders were coming down from Bobby. Where my case was concerned, I *know* all red tape had to be cleared through him. I'm not naive—he hated my guts. During the McClellan hearings, after I'd taken the Fifth Amendment 142 straight times, Bobby was fit to be tied. In that high-pitched, bean-and-cod-accented voice of his, his reaction was typical: "With the records we have, we'll prove what Beck would have said if he had talked." Bobby Kennedy was just a very ambitious young man. If his objective was to play God over me, he wasn't successful because he never worried me one bit. Perhaps he felt he could destroy me once and for all by putting me in prison, I don't know. I *do* know, however, that I think I have a finer public image today than I ever had prior to going to jail. So if Bobby Kennedy's intent was to crush my spirit, he failed abysmally.

McCallum:

On March 11, 1963, the grim information that Dave Beck had been dreading was distributed to him over telephone wire, publicized by Seattle radio stations, and confirmed in newspaper print: "Rosary for Mrs. Mary Beck, 94, mother of former Teamsters boss Dave Beck, will be held tonight in Seattle. Requiem Mass will be sung tomorrow. Beck has told officials at McNeil Island Penitentiary that he will not attend the services. Warden Paul Madigan said he would be allowed to attend if he wished. Mrs. Beck was born in San Francisco. She had lived in Seattle since 1898."

The *Seattle Times* printed a lengthy account of the Mary Beck funeral. But the edition containing the article was three days old before son Dave, lying abed in his cell, got around to reading it. The fact he did not attend his own mother's funeral surprised many of his friends. He'd loved her deeply, had been dedicated to her. What was the story?

Beck:

Pride. Foolish pride. As soon as I was told she had died, I went to McNeil authorities and asked them to grant me permission to attend the funeral. They said, "Yes"—with one proviso. A prison guard would be required to go with me. I said, "No, no guard. I'm not giving the press a field day. I'm too well known. I can see the headlines now: DAVE BECK ATTENDS MOTHER'S FUNERAL IN HANDCUFFS. No, siree, I'm going by myself, or I'm not going. Have some compassion."

To illustrate how our government changes, a couple of years later after Jimmy Hoffa was sent to prison, he was allowed to fly to his wife's bedside in San Francisco for 30 days. *All by himself.* But in my case, during the Kennedy Administration, that was impossible. I didn't beef. I simply told the prison officials I wouldn't go. They tried to placate me by pointing out that the guard had orders to stay out of sight at the funeral so as not to embarrass me. I said to forget it, they were wasting their time. I wasn't sure as hell going to create another sensational news angle for reporters at my own mother's burial. While the McNeil authorities listened, I phoned my sister, Reta, and told her I wouldn't be coming to the services. My sister agreed. I loved my mother very much. It was a helluva way to say goodbye to her.

McCallum:

The distance between McNeil Island and Seattle is approximately 35 miles. To Dave Beck, it seemed more like a hundred miles. On February 20, 1964, after serving one third of his five-year federal sentence, he came up for parole, but the Federal Parole Board, without comment, denied his bid for freedom. A Justice Department spokesman refused to elaborate. But investigative reporters close to the case knew without being told that Beck lost his chance for early release when he was banished to solitary confinement. It cost him 30 days of time off for good behavior.

Five months later, the question of Beck's parole popped up again. Reported the Associated Press:

> If and when Beck is paroled, he must await action by the Washington State Board of Prison Terms and Paroles. He is still technically under a 3-year sentence on a state charge of selling a Teamster-owned automobile for $1,900 and pocketing the money. The state conviction followed the federal trial, and both convictions were upheld by higher courts after a long series of legal maneuvers. The state board has agreed to let Beck's federal and state sentences be served concurrently and set his minimum term at two years. Therefore, with "good time" credit, Beck technically has been eligible for parole from his state sentence since last October. The state board has indicated Beck would probably be paroled simultaneously with his release from McNeil Island.

When Beck first went into McNeil, he had no idea when he would be getting out, but after 30 months he began to see the sunlight at the end of the tunnel. One day on his way from the cannery, he met Frankie Carbo, the old underworld boss of prizefighting during the 1930s, '40s, and '50s. Carbo was at McNeil because he had once attempted to muscle in on half of the earnings of world welterweight champion Don Jordan. He was tried and convicted in federal court in 1961 of conspiracy and extortion and got 25 years. (Carbo died in the federal pen in 1975.)

Carbo told Beck he had been hearing rumors.

"What rumors?" Beck wanted to know.

"According to my sources," Carbo said, "you're getting out of here."

"Several cons have told me the same thing. But I don't believe them."

"It's the truth, Dave. You're getting out. It's all set."

Carbo usually had the straight dope. You could bank your life on his sources of information. He got his information in ways known only to himself.

"Don't ask me how I know or who gave me the tip," Carbo said. "But you're going home."

Beck:

I went back to my cell. By evening, the rumors were flying all over the island. *Dave Beck is being paroled.* I was skeptical, however, because I still hadn't heard from anyone in authority. Then my caseworker phoned and said he wanted to see me in his office. "Right now," he said. There was a sense of urgency in his voice. I thought, "This is it. I'm going home."

The caseworker looked at me glumly.

"There's a rumor going around that you're being released," he began. "Surely you've heard it."

"I don't know a thing," I said. "All I know is what you know. I've had at least nine guys stop me today and say I'm going out."

The caseworker's mouth formed into a smirk.

"Well," he said, "don't believe what you hear. You're staying."

He seemed to be gloating. I didn't particularly like him. In fact, I don't even remember his name. He never made much of an impression on me. I said to him, "Hey, now, wait a minute. I'm not going to argue with you over a couple of rumors. But the fact remains that the wire services, the radio, and TV networks are all spreading the news that the parole board is sending me home. They must know something—and I've had a helluva lot more experience dealing with the news media than you'll ever have. I'm inclined to believe them. You think what you want."

"Well, we're not going to pay attention to the reports until they're official. Huh? Well, *are* we?"

"Do what you want," I told him.

The next morning, the caseworker called me out of the cannery at 10 o'clock. "It's official," he said. "In 10 days you're getting out of here."

That's all he said. He sounded disappointed.

The news had no exceptional impact on me. I slept no better that night than I had the other 900 nights I'd been at McNeil—and I'd slept well most of the time.

McCallum:

December 2, 1964. Newspaper headlines told the story: FEDS GIVE DAVE BECK PAROLE FOR YULE PRESENT. "Dave Beck, the laundry truck driver who rose to become the millionaire chief of the Teamsters Union, is scheduled to leave the prison on parole, December 11," reported the *Tacoma News Tribune.* "Prison officials said Beck probably would leave on the 10:30 a.m. boat to Steilacoom, touching 'free soil' for the first time in more than two years at about 10:55 a.m. The bouncy, round-faced Beck, now 70, was granted the parole by the U.S. Parole Board Tuesday and will be under the supervision of a federal probation officer in Seattle until his sentence expires, June 20, 1967. A three-year state parole also starts when Beck steps off McNeil Island. He will be under supervision of the state board once his federal sentence is complete."

The Associated Press quoted a McNeil spokesman as saying that Beck was entitled to transportation money to Seattle, a "gratuity" to cover meals and expenses while en route, any money he earned in prison, and a brand new, prison-made suit.

Beck:

I never got a cent for the time I served and worked at McNeil. Nor did I get a free suit and the customary $5 when I left the Island. Ten days before I got out, I was told to report to the prison tailor to be measured for my going-away suit. As the tailor took his tape and started to put it around my middle, I looked at him and said, "You're wasting your time."

"Why?"

"Because I'm not going to wear the suit home."

"You aren't?"

"No. I'm having a suit sent over from home."

"Then you can't have this suit."

"The hell I can't."

"What do you want it for? You just said you're not going to wear it."

"I want it to drop over the side of the boat when I ride away from this goddamn place."

"You can't do that."

"Then I'll give it to the Salvation Army."

"No, no, no."

P.S. They never did give me that goddamn going-away suit.

McCallum:

December 11, 1964. For Beck, checking out of McNeil was reminiscent of getting out of the Navy. There was clothing to turn in, equipment to return, a medical checkup, and other administrative details to be completed before he was allowed to return to the mainland and freedom. Despite his reputation, he was, as the warden explained, "being processed out of the prison in the same manner as every other prisoner." The routine also included stops at the hospital for clearance, the fiscal office, the library, education center, and hobby shop; then back to his cell for one last time to wait for McNeil's iron gates to swing open, and finally the short ride back to the mainland.

The day was bright and crisp, and a chill wind blew in across the salt water from the north. Beck wore sunglasses, a blue serge suit, and a dark hat. He had lost none of the bounce in his walk. After 30 months, he was happy to be going home.

And then he saw the boats offshore.

Beck:

I was waiting in the dock's little waiting room for the signal to board the prison boat when I first noticed this boat circling around and around in front of McNeil. The Coast Guard was supposed to patrol those waters. After all, such an unidentified craft might have been there to aid an escape, for all the authorities knew.

I was still trying to figure why it was there, when this guard stepped up to me and said, "I have never met you, Mr. Beck. Let's go out on the veranda and talk."

I pointed to the mysterious boat.

"What's it doing out there?" I asked. "Why is it circling back and forth? What do they want?"

He shook his head. "I don't know."

"Well," I said, "D'ya know what I think? I think it's filled with photographers with telescopic lenses to take pictures of me for tonight's papers. No, sir, I'm not going outside with you."

The guard appeared puzzled.

"Listen," I told him. "It's your duty to call the Coast Guard and alert them; find out if that boat has authorization to be there."

His only reply was to walk away.

The boat kept circling. When it came time to get aboard, I draped my topcoat over my head so that those photographers with their long-range lenses couldn't get a clear shot of my face. I had been through scenes like this before and knew what to do. There were about 10 other men coming off the Island with me, half of them black.

Halfway to the mainland, this guard came up to me and said, "Mr. Beck, you'll be the first one off the boat."

"Oh, no," I told him. "I'm going to be the *last* one off. You see that boat out there? What's it doing?"

He said, "I don't know."

I said, "The hell you don't. If you don't know what it's doing, you're dumber than I think you are."

"Now wait a minute," he protested. "You're not out of here yet."

"Oh, yes I am," I said. "Who told you to tell me to walk off of here first?"

"Those are my orders."

"Well," I said, "forget it. I'm not going off first. When I came down that gangplank at the prison dock, I was officially out of McNeil. So I don't have to take orders from you—and I'm telling you I'm getting off *last*."

"First," insisted the guard. "You're going first."

One of the black men overheard the argument, and he said, "Mr. Beck, you want us to throw him overboard?"

Of course, I was right about the mystery boat. It was loaded with cameramen and photographers. Three of the Seattle TV stations and the two newspapers had joined forces and chartered it. But I had my way; I got off the boat last—five minutes after all the other passengers. Yet there was no avoiding the news guys. As I walked up the dock, there must have been at least 50 waiting to greet me and to ask questions. It was so crowded that they got into a pushing match and one of the photographers slipped into the bay. I brushed right past them all without a word and got into a car, where my son and attorney were waiting.

And *that* is how Dave Beck left McNeil Island.

That night, it was all on the TV news. I thought I'd die laughing when I saw that photographer fall into the water. It was better even than Howdy Doody.

13
The
Pardon

BATTEN down the hatches. Beck was back. The next day, he talked to the press.

"How was the food?" someone wanted to know.

"Great," Beck said. "I'm telling you, every morning we had breakfasts fit for a king. Orange juice, grapefruit, fruits of all kinds several times a week; hotcakes and ham and eggs at least three times a week; hot cereal, cold cereal, take your pick. Believe me, we had better food than most of you get out here."

Another reporter asked about the guards. Did Beck get along with them? On the whole, he said, he found them to be all right. "Not at all sadistic," he said. "Not in the least like they are portrayed on TV and in the movies. Oh, there were a couple of bastards among them; bullies who let us know pretty roughly that they were boss and to do what they said or go on report. I ignored them. If they hassled me, I told them, 'Now, wait a minute, Mister. If I'm breaking a prison rule, take me to the warden and let *him* tell me what I'm doing wrong.' They usually left me alone. I had very little trouble with them."

What was his life like at McNeil? What did he do with himself?

"Lots of reading," he said. "I watched TV, listened to the radio, and spent a lot of time in the library. I had a job in the cannery, supervisor; four people under me. I liked it. Fights, sexual attacks, drugs—I never saw any of it. Oh, sure, I heard rumblings that those things went on, but I never saw it. Frankly, I never saw a single, solitary fight in all the time I was there. I saw arguments and emotions erupt but never to the point of an explosion. There were just too many cool heads around to let things get out of hand."

The other inmates, how did he get along with them?

"All right," Beck said. "Sure, there were some damn tough palookas—con artists, thieves, murderers, bootleggers, dope smugglers, draft dodgers—but there were also some very fine fellows. I wanted to help the good ones but couldn't because prison rules wouldn't let me."

Jimmy Hoffa. Was he pleased with the way Hoffa was running the Teamsters?

"He's doing a good job."

Bobby Kennedy?

"I do not care to comment on him. He has problems of his own."

As to his views of the rest of prison life, except for the stigma of having been in a federal penitentiary, Beck recommended it for all overweight businessmen. "Throw away all those health ads," he said. "Look at me. I weighed 209 when I went to McNeil, now I'm a bony 168. If I can reduce on prison food, anyone can."

Today, 14 years later, Beck still goes to great lengths to put his conviction into perspective and to defend his honor. For example, whenever he feels a publication has taken a cheap shot at him or misrepresents the facts of his case, he shoots off a letter demanding a retraction or a clarification. "I have no skeletons in my closet," he says. "My life is an open book. S'help me, I hope my mother's soul goes to hell and stays there until eternity if I'm not telling the truth."

Beck:

I have had Congressmen ask me, "Dave, why did you insist on a Presidential pardon?" My reply always has been the same. "Because I wanted my American citizenship restored." In World War I, I volunteered for military duty overseas, and in my opinion, I have always been a good American. Granted, I have fought with politicians and labor leaders and big businessmen and academicians; and I loudly disagreed with people on the question of communism when I was head of the Board of Regents at University of Washington. But I never purposely broke the law. So in view of my past record, I insisted on a full pardon from the President so that my voting rights and American citizenship could be restored.

I made a regular, routine application to President Johnson for a pardon, but I never got anywhere. I never attempted to put any pressure on him. Hell, I never had any confidence in his integrity, anyway. He was strictly a politician. Oh, labor got a fair enough deal from him; it's just that, personally, there will always be a question mark whether there was any truth involving Johnson in what later developed into the Bobby Baker scandal.

Now for the irony of the bottom line:

When my pardon finally came through in 1976, it was signed by a Republican President (Gerald Ford)—with an anti-labor record as bad as you can get.

14

Mr. Beck: An Insider's View

ANN Watkins Kotin grew up in a small town outside of Seattle and now lives in Los Angeles with her husband, who is in labor relations. On a recent trip to the Queen City, she settled herself in a big, lumpy easy chair in Dave Beck's apartment and reminisced. Dave sat across the room in his favorite soft, leather chair and listened. For 31 years they'd worked together as boss and private secretary, Ann said, and now, well, it was as though they had never been away. Dave nodded. Yes, he said, it was great fun to be talking about the good old days again, when the world was younger, if not better.

Until the day he retired, Dave was always "Mister Beck," to Ann. Then, one day, while cleaning up some old papers, he telephoned her to come and help him. They were reviewing some incident, and Ann said, "Well, Mr. Beck—" and Dave interrupted her and said, "Why don't you call me Dave?"

For a moment, Ann was frustrated.

"I don't think I possibly can," she told him. "A habit of 31 years is hard to break."

"Well, try," Dave said.

That evening, she went home and told her husband about her mental block. He said he could appreciate her diffidence.

Now this was 1978 and Ann was enjoying the details.

"I went back to Dave and told him, 'All right, I'll call you Dave. But I'm not comfortable with it.' Well, I called him DB, and I called him Mister Beck, but I never could bring myself to call him Dave. Even now I hesitate, after all these years. You may hear me call him Dave, yet I'm still thinking Mister Beck."

Dave perked up. Ann's story about person-to-person familiarity had reminded him of an incident involving his sister years ago.

"My sister was living in Baltimore when her husband died," he said. "I sent my wife, Dorothy, back to bring her and her young daughter back to the Northwest to live. For some time, I put her up at a summer place we had over on Bainbridge Island. There she grew bored with idleness and asked to go to work. I first got her a job with the Port Commission; then I put her to work as a telephone operator in our Teamster building in Seattle. One morning, I came into the front entrance as she was talking to some of the secretaries and office help. I was just about to round the corner to go up to my office, when she called after me, 'Dave!' I decided to have a little fun with her. I wheeled around and went back to her. I looked her squarely in the eyes and, with a straight face, I said, 'What did you call me?' She said, 'I called you Dave.' I growled, 'Listen, you're an employee in this building, the same as everyone else. I'm running this International Union in this building and it's "Mister Beck" to you and everybody else during working hours.' She was plainly stunned. Then I did a quick pivot and started for my office again. I was just about out of sight when she shouted at me again: '*Mister* Beck!' I came back once more. 'What is it you want now?' She said, 'I just want to say to you— you *sonofabitch!*' You can appreciate the story if you know that my sister seldom swore. I was a year living that down. The story quickly went around the building and whenever I'd meet one of the fellows in the hall, he'd grin and say, 'Hey, you sonofabitch.'"

The conversation grew serious. Ann said the sharpest image she had of Dave Beck in his prime was that he was a man of vision, a tireless worker, totally dedicated to the cause. He would spend his evenings at home writing endless pages of memos to himself on long, yellow legal pads; notes he would turn over to her the next day to be typed up; ideas he had for the Teamsters.

"He didn't say to himself, 'If I do this, what is it going to mean today, or tomorrow, or next week, or next month?'" she said. "It was more like, 'What is it going to mean six months from now, a year from now, *five* years from now?' He had a swift mind. New ideas were always developing in it. He never seemed to get tired. Long 16-18-hour days were not uncommon, to him. His wife, Dorothy, once told me that there was something unusual about his recuperative powers. 'When he comes home,' she said, 'it might be 10 minutes before dinner, and he can sit down in a chair and sleep for eight minutes. He can relax that quickly.'"

Thoughtful for a moment, Ann chuckled. Dave, watching her, wanted to know what was tickling her funny bone. Oh, she said, did he remember the only time she visited him at McNeil Island? Now Dave laughed, his face turning red.

"Well," she said, turning to me, "I told Dave the night before he turned himself over to the U.S. Marshal to begin serving his sentence, that I was coming over to see him. He refused to permit his mother or sister to come, but he knew better than to try and stop me. When he broke the news that he was leaving for McNeil the next day, I started to cry. He said, 'Now, wait a minute; get control of yourself. This is going to lengthen my life by 10 years. Don't worry about a thing. I will be all right.' I told him, 'Well, Mr.

Beck, I'm going to come to see you. Wild horses can't stop me.' And he said, 'Knowing you as well as I do, when you say you are going to do something, you do it.'

"Well, the day came when I took the prison boat over to McNeil. It was very strange. I mean, the guards just let me walk through the gate. They never searched me, didn't even check my handbag. The guards must have thought Dave and I were insane, because we sat at this round table in the visitor's room talking about the old days and laughing ourselves silly.

"On the boat going over, I was asked if I had made arrangements for lunch. I said I didn't know anything about prison protocol and guessed that Dave would see to it I was fed. So while Dave and I talked, a lunch cart on wheels rolled by. Dave went over and took two box lunches, coffee, silverware, and napkins and brought them back to our table. Then, in picnic fashion, he carefully set two places. After we finished eating, he gathered up the debris, carried it over to a trashcan and deposited it, and came back. Then he looked at me, and said, 'Well, Ann, you can't say I never took you to lunch.'"

Dave picked up the mood with a story of his own.

"I don't think I ever told you, Ann, but there was this entertainer we used to hire for Teamster functions," Dave said. "He also used to book whole shows for us. He once got us an act comprised of a little boy, his father, and uncle; we got all three of them for $70. The little boy's name was—Sammy Davis, Jr. Now, you couldn't get him for $10,000 a night. So when I was at McNeil, this guy, the booking agent, showed up with an act to entertain the inmates. He knew I was there and tried to find me. The only way he could talk to me was through channels, and the guards wouldn't tell him how to find me. He probably wanted me to use my influence to get him more Teamster bookings. Anyway, he walked out on the stage at McNeil to introduce the first act, and the first thing he said was, 'Is there anybody in the audience who knows Ann Watkins?' When I stood up, he said, 'I'll see you after the show.' Now he knew where Dave Beck was. When he said he'd see me after the show, the authorities damn near ran him off the Island."

Ann said, "I once phoned the prison and told the man who answered that if it was possible for him to get a message to Mr. Beck, to please tell him that my brother had just died and that I was in Seattle for the funeral and I just wanted him to know. The man said, 'Not only will I see that he gets the message, I'll hang up this phone and will go directly, personally, to him and make sure he gets the information,' I thought to myself, 'Boy, Mr. Beck must have some sort of status in there to have them jumping so.' Soon after, he wrote me a letter about my brother's death and about life and death; it was the most beautiful letter I have ever received."

On the subject of prison, I asked Ann what she knew about the events leading up to Beck's conviction. She said she was questioned in the federal courthouse in Seattle. "I was asked if I ever saw the annual report," she said. "I recall saying that anything that went on Mr. Beck's desk for his signature I saw and knew about. I had a habit of going in to his desk every morning and sorting his mail so that the important letters were over here, the next important things were here, and the scruffy stuff was over there. In other words, I normally *saw* what was on his desk. But the annual report in question had nothing to do with me for the simple reason that I was working for Mr. Beck in Washington, D.C. at the time, not the Seattle office, where the mistake occurred. So I was not a part of it."

"Ann was not a part of it at all," Beck said. "Marcella Guiry was my secretary in my Seattle office then. And she swore she never saw the annual report. Brewster and McDonald, our Seattle bookkeeper, testified that they came upstairs and put the report on my desk. Marcella testified that she never saw it. And it was not signed by me. Who mailed it back to Washington, I don't know. Marcella and I had a terrible argument with her attorney over the facts. It's all in the transcript of the trial over in

Tacoma. Her attorney tried to get Marcella to go into court and make any statement that would clear her. I insisted that she go in and just tell the *truth*."

I said, "Dave, the government must have wanted you awfully bad."

"Of course, Beck said.

"Obviously, somebody was out to make an example of you," I said.

"Of course," Beck said.

Ann said, "You just wouldn't believe the things they did to build a case against Mr. Beck."

"You can have your opinion," Beck said. "I have mine."

"What do you feel was going through their minds?" I asked. "Since we can't nail him for this, or this, or this, we'll get him for this, they seemed to be saying."

"That's exactly right," Beck said. "They convicted me on a technicality, and they made it stick."

Ann said she wanted to change the subject. After 20 years, she said, it still makes her bitter.

"No," Dave said. "I also want to clear up the matter of the Cadillac. I'm talking about the car that was owned by the Joint Council of Teamsters in Seattle, and as president of the Joint Council I used it whenever I was here. Then someone came along while I was in Washington and told Marcella they wanted to buy it. They gave her a check and she phoned me long-distance and said she'd deposited the check in the International Brotherhood of Teamsters' account. I told her, 'No, Marcella, that's wrong. The Cadillac is not owned by the International Brotherhood of Teamsters, it's not owned by me, it's owned by the Joint Council. So then she turned around and deposited the check in my own personal account, which I just got through telling her didn't belong there. So when I came back to Seattle and it was brought to my attention, I immediately paid back the $1,900 out of my own personal funds to the Joint Council. There was no argument about that. So when the case went to the Grand Jury, a member of the jury asked

me where the money was. I told him it was in the safe
deposit box of the Joint Council. 'All right,' he asked, 'may
we go over and look at it?' 'Of course,' I said. And several of
them went to the office, opened the safe deposit box, and
there was the money. That's the truth, too. Yet the State
convicted me on the charge of selling the Cadillac and
pocketing the money. You figure it out."

"Ann," I asked, "what was it like working for Dave?
Was he terribly tough? Did you ever fight?"

"When the Becks were getting ready to go to Europe
for the first time—I think it was 1949—on Friday, which
was the end of that working week, all the fellows wanted to
see Mr. Beck—everybody seemed to want to talk to him at
once. He had a lot of dictation still to give me, so I said to
him, 'Look, Mr. Beck, instead of your trying to see all these
people today and dictating those letters, we can do the
letters on Saturday. Suppose I come down to the office
tomorrow and you give me the dictation and then we won't
worry about anything but seeing the fellows today. So Sam
Bassett, our attorney, was in Mr. Beck's office, and it was
about two o'clock when Mr. Beck got this telephone call.
After he hung up, he called me on the intercom and
shouted, 'Did you see a letter from so-and-so?' I said, yes,
it came across my desk and I answered it. 'Come in here,'
he snapped. This was the only time this man was ever really
mad at me, and he let it out. He laid me out and told me
I shouldn't have done what I did, and what in the world
was I thinking about? In my defense, I said, 'I thought I
was doing the right thing.' He waved me out of the room. I
sat down at my desk and was very shaken. Gordon Lind-
sey came into the office, saw my despair, and asked, 'Ann,
are you all right? Are you ill?' I told him I was fine. 'Then
why are you white as a sheet?' he wanted to know. I said,
'No, no, Gordon, I'm fine. Really.' Then Sam Bassett, who
had witnessed the explosion, walked out of Mr. Beck's office and said to me, 'Ann, don't feel badly. I'm a lawyer,
and if I had been handling the situation, I would have done
exactly as you did. You did the right thing.'

"For the rest of the afternoon, there was not another peep out of Mr. Beck. But at 5 p.m., he walked out of his office, put on his coat and hat, got as far as the front doorknob, and paused. He turned and looked at me and his face was as red as a tomato. 'Are you still coming in here tomorrow morning?' I said, 'Of course. I said I would. Of course, I am.'

"Next day, we both arrived at the office at the same time. We dived head first into our work and were well into it, when all of a sudden he stopped. Out of the blue he said, 'Beginning this month, you're getting $100 a month raise.' I said, 'What? Mr. Beck, the money is very nice, but the fact that you feel this way is more important.' And he said, 'Well, you *earn* it.'"

Another Beck story? "Let's see," Ann said. Yes, it had to do with that January afternoon, 1958, when the court came down with a decision permitting Jimmy Hoffa to finally take over as president of the International Union under the board of monitors. Ann remembered that Beck buzzed her on the office intercom, and said, "Ann, get me a ticket on the first possible flight to Seattle." Just like that. He was moving back home. She managed to reserve him a ticket on a plane that was leaving at 1:30 p.m. As she sat at her desk, waiting for Beck to leave, it suddenly dawned on Ann that, by gosh, the end of their 31 years together was at hand.

"I was just floating around in a fog somewhere," she said, "on the brink of tears. On his way out of the office, Dave went around the room saying goodby to the staff. Finally, he turned and saw the tears welling up in my eyes. 'What's the matter with you, Ann?' he asked. I snapped, 'You know what's the matter with me? You don't have to ask me a dumb question like that.' 'Listen,' he said, whirling around and pointing a finger at me. 'When you came to work for me, nobody promised you a *permanent* job.'"

One day, she continued, she was in his office taking dictation. The year was either 1948 or '49, and a tall TV tower had just been erected at Denny Way and Taylor on the other side of the Teamsters building in Seattle.

"I had an appointment downtown at noon and about five minutes to 12 he called me in to take down this letter," she said. "I thought that was cutting it pretty short, dictating a letter so close to the lunch hour. But I went in, took my seat, prepared to write. All of a sudden the room began to shake. Earthquake! The worst one in the state's history. Cornices fell off of the buildings, streets buckled, windows shattered, cracks appeared in the earth. The center of the quake was in Olympia. Dave had four lighting fixtures hanging from the ceiling and they were swaying back and forth like a trapeze. I was petrified. I had just read a book about the nightmarish 1923 earthquake in Japan; I knew if I looked out the window, the earth would open up and just swallow us whole. I glanced outdoors and that TV tower was going like a buggywhip, whiplashing to and fro. I looked over at Dave for moral support, and all he said was, 'Oh, it's just a *little* earthquake.' *His* sense of humor."

Ann recalled that, year after year, on October 3rd, she would remind her boss that she had been with him for five years, or 10 years, or 20 years, or whatever. In 1957 they were attending the Teamsters convention in Miami Beach, and as Dave, Dorothy, and Ann were driving to the banquet, she, Ann, who was sitting in the back seat, said to Dave, "You know something, Mr. Beck? Today I have been working for you for 30 years." All he said was, "Oh, is that so?" Big deal. Later, during the program, Ann was sitting at the head table lost in her job, and Dave got up and started to address the audience. As he talked, Ann took notes. Suddenly, Dave stopped, and turned to Ann. He called her to the podium. Taking her by the hand, he turned back to his fellow Teamsters and said: "Thirty years ago, today, she went to work for me." There was a long pause, then: "I sure can pick 'em, can't I?"

George Vanderveer, the late attorney? Yes, she said, George was as colorful as Mr. Beck described him. "Once," she said, "he was in court defending a client who was being sued by a woman injured in a car wreck. The victim sup-

posedly was incapacitated from the waist down. She
couldn't walk, had no feeling in her legs. She was wheeled
into the court room and testified from a wheelchair. George
was standing alongside her as he questioned her. Hidden in
one hand was a pin. Suddenly he jabbed it in her leg, she
let out a shattering scream—and there went her ironclad
case. Not much got by George Vanderveer."

"When I first met George," Dave said, "he was an attorney for the Wobblies, our arch rivals in those early days.
I was always opposed to them, but slowly George came
around to our thinking and wound up working for me."

Inevitably, the conversation swung around to Jimmy
Hoffa. Yes, Ann said, she had some opinions about him,
too.She told about an incident she had with him following
a convention in Seattle in 1957, when she wrote a formal
memo announcing that she was leaving the Teamsters.

"My husband had come out to Los Angeles almost two
years before and was waiting for me to join him," Ann said.
"My marriage hinged on going to California. But my pension was in question. Johnny English, secretary-treasurer
of the union, just wasn't about to give me my retirement
pension. He obviously was trying to be nasty with Dave
Beck, and he knew that if he hurt me, he would be hurting
Dave. So here was Hoffa, listening to my woes, and he said,
'Ann, if anybody in this International Union has a retirement coming, you are the one. If you will stay with me for
two months—just two months during the transition—I will
see that you get the whole thing.' The public never saw
that side of Jimmy, but he could be a very gentle, very
sweet man; and with all this gentleness, this sweetness, it
was hard to talk negatively about him—especially when it
came to his deep relationship with his family. He was a
wonderful family man. I don't know, but I don't think you
can write him off as *all* bad. Am I right, Dave?"

"I still must fault Jimmy for not showing the nerve to
tell Johnny English off when he, Hoffa, was sitting on the
board as a vice-president," Beck said. "He took a lot of guff

because he wanted English's support when he ran for president. He should have stood up to Johnny English more."

"Hoffa had a very sharp mind," Ann said. "Once, in our Washington office—I'll never forget—Hoffa and Dave had been in a meeting. When it broke up, Jimmy had to rush to catch a plane for Detroit. He was late. He got as far as the door, one hand on the knob, when one of the office staff shouted after him, 'Jimmy, what about so-and-so; what do you want us to do?' Jimmy hesitated at the door, and he recited all the technicalities of a labor agreement out of his head and all the machinations of the negotiations involved; whipped them out just like that. He really had a razor-sharp brain. Didn't he, Dave?"

"Oh, yes, he was able," Beck said. "He made only one mistake. He got in with the wrong people and let them get inside the tent with him."

"Yes, I think so," Ann agreed. "I think that is what happened. It probably dated all the way back to his boyhood."

"I really don't know what Hoffa's connections were," Beck said. "An insurance investor once came to see me. He had a letter of introduction from Hoffa and he had been investing for Jimmy up in Detroit. I asked Einar Mohn to sit in on the meeting, so there would be a witness to the conversation. The fellow wanted to handle our investment money. I heard him out and then said I was sorry. I told him, 'I have no objections to how they invest their money up in Detroit, that's their money. Hoffa can invest it any way his people will support him, but you're never going to invest a dollar of this money out of this office.' That's why I keep saying, I don't know what Hoffa's connections were in the field of investments."

Ann was very fond of Dorothy Beck. She was the kind of wife, Ann explained, who never came to the office except when it was absolutely necessary. She rarely even phoned the office. She was a warm, wonderful lady, Ann said.

"Once, many years ago, Dave wanted me to audit the

books in Astoria, Oregon," Ann said. "So the three of us drove down. While I worked on the books, Dave and Dorothy took a little drive down to Seaside. When they got back, it was decided that Dorothy and I would drive back to Seattle together, because Dave had to catch a plane from Portland to San Francisco on some urgent business. As we drove up Highway 99, I said, 'Mrs. Beck—' and she said, 'Ann, call me *Dorothy*.' That was a big compliment, putting our relationship on a first-name basis. I said, 'Dorothy, do you get lonely? Does it bother you a lot when Mr. Beck is away so much of the time?' I will never forget her answer. 'Ann,' she replied, 'when it's your bread and butter, you don't complain.'

"For Dorothy, the end came suddenly. Dave was giving me dictation. Always, he sat on his side of the desk and I took a chair across from him. He was dictating a letter to Dan Tobin, who had asked Dave to bring Dorothy to Miami Beach. Dave was telling Dan that he was sorry, but they couldn't come. He was in the middle of a sentence when all of a sudden his voice choked. It just closed up tight; emotion drained his face. He got out of his chair, walked around the desk behind me, wiped the tears from his eyes, then continued: 'The doctor tells me that Dorothy is too sick to travel.' He could hardly say the words, they hurt so badly.

"She died only a few days after she entered the hospital. It was a combination of asthma and a heart condition. The doctor had told Dave she was doing fine. Then, the day after Thanksgiving, 1961, it ended. I had been in Seattle on a visit for a few days, and Fred Lordan and I had lunch at the Olympic Hotel. Getting up from the table, Fred asked, 'What are you going to do?' I told him, 'I think I will walk across the street and see Dr. Alexander Grinstein.' I went over and knocked on his private door but he wasn't in. I waited. Presently, he arrived and his face was filled with pain. 'What is it, Doctor?' I asked. He looked at me as he had never looked at me before. He went over and sat down. Finally, he spoke. 'Ann,' he said, 'I have some sad news for you.' I said, 'It's Dorothy, isn't it?' because I knew she was in the hospital. Dr. Grinstein adored her. 'Yes,' he said. 'It is Dorothy.' He put his head in his hands and stared at the floor. 'She just died.' Tears filled his eyes, then, in a whisper, 'This is a helluva way to make a living.'"

15
Wheeler, Dealer

Y ES, I guess you can say Dave Beck is hard-nosed when it comes to real estate," the man said. "When you ask him to reduce a price, he'll tell you, 'I've never reduced a price on a piece of property in my life. Take it or leave it.' To my knowledge, he *never* has come down in price; if it doesn't sell in six months, *up* goes the price. That's Dave Beck, for you."

As he speaks, Pat Metzger, tall, white-haired, and Irish, gestures languidly with hands as big as shovels, as if trying to shape the words in the air. He came out of the little mining town of Kellogg, Idaho, majored in journalism at the University of Idaho, and for the past 20 years has been a successful realtor in Seattle. He met Beck in 1973 through property transactions.

"I will tell you about a 330-acre farm that Dave and three associates bought many years ago," Pat continued. "They paid $40,000 for it originally; purchased it for a hunting and fishing retreat. Then Dave's partners wanted out, and he bought their interests. One day, Dave told me about this property at Cathcart, Washington. I asked him what he was asking for it, and he said $1,000 an acre. I told him, 'That comes to $330,000. I'll go out and look at it.' So I drove out and looked at the property. I parked the car off the road, and by the time I had walked 50 feet and looked at this farm, there must have been at least three feet of water over the whole 330 acres. I thought, my god, what does he farm—water? For $1,000 an acre, there was a flood in there at least once, sometimes twice a year, and I told myself, Beck is absolutely crazy. Anyway, I showed the property to other people and they agreed with me. So I came back to Dave and asked him if he would be willing to come down in his price. He said, 'No way.' After 20 years in the business, I thought I knew real estate pretty well; apparently, I don't. Dave just sold the farm for $375,000!

"I tell you, Dave Beck doesn't come down in price; he goes up in price. Talk about finesse. I deal with *big* real estate investors, but none more hard-nosed than Dave. I guess you could say that I could sell him anything he could steal. I say that guardedly, meaning he would have to be able to buy a property below the market so he could sell it above the market. That's why he has achieved such great success in real estate."

Beck was sitting at the other end of the room as I talked to Pat. He had just gotten off the telephone regarding the sale of another piece of property. He was busy jotting down some figures on a yellow legal pad.

"Dave?" Pat asked him.

Beck looked up from his numbers.

"Yes?"

"What was the first piece of property you ever bought?"

"Let's see," Dave said, thoughtfully. "That would be my home out on 5752 27th Avenue N.E. From Mr. Whitney, I bought the lot and then I had him agree to give me title to the lot."

"How did you buy it?" Pat wanted to know.

Dave Beck at the time he was president of the University of Washington Board of Regents. While he was president, the Husky Stadium was expanded to its present size, the Conibear Shell House was constructed and today's modern medical school and hospital complex was begun.   Photo: Bachrach

Ann Watkins Kotin, Dave Beck's secretary for 31 years, responds with Dave to the Teamsters at their International Convention in 1957 on the occasion of their joint retirement.

Mary Tierney Beck, Dave's mother—the mainstay of his life until her death at 94 in 1963.

Dave Beck heads for McNeil Island in 1962.

Photo: *Tacoma News Tribune*

Dave Beck returning from McNeil Island Penitentiary in 1964.

Photo: *Tacoma News Tribune*

Seattle home of Dave Beck purchased by the Teamsters as his presidential residence.

Dave and Helen Beck, his second wife for ten years, at Butchart Gardens, Victoria, British Columbia, 1973.

Dave Beck and his sister, Reta, outside her home in Sheridan Beach near Seattle.

Dave working out on his exercise cycle, a daily habit for many years in good and bad weather.   Photo: *Tacoma News Tribune*

"By paying $10 or $15 down and $10 or $20 a month until it was all paid for. I had Mr. Whitney give me title to the property in order to get a mortgage loan for it, which I secured from the Washington Mutual Bank, and it continued on until I paid off the mortgage."

"Do you remember the size of the mortgage?"

"About $1,800."

"So your first house didn't exceed $2,500?"

"No. But that's as good as a $60,000 house by today's values."

"But you were paying upwards of $10 a month on your land and about $25 monthly on your mortgage?"

"Yes."

"What were your interest rates?" Pat wanted to know.

"About 4½ percent, I think" Beck answered.

"What year was that?"

"In 1923, I believe."

"And when you moved out of that house, you sold it."

"Yes," Beck said, "plus two additional adjoining lots I bought later under the same financial arrangements."

"What was the gross sale?"

"I think I sold it for $17,000—after living in the house for about 20 years," Beck said.

"Dave," Pat said, "did you really live in a $2,500 house for 27 years?"

"That's right."

"And sold it for $17,000?"

"Yes."

"And that gave you—that was your first inclination of how you could make money in real estate?"

"I was always of the opinion, after buying the very first house, that I could make money in real estate," Beck said.

"What was your next purchase?" asked Pat.

"Out at Sheridan Beach, at 16749 Shore Drive, in the northend," Beck replied.

"Actually," Pat said, "that was where you really got started in real estate, wasn't it?"

"Yes. Oh, wait. I had other transactions before. I bought property from the same Mr. Whitney, right back of us on 28th Avenue N.E.; and I bought another lot on the corner above it and built a house for my mother and sister."

"And you did as well on those houses as you did on your own?"

"Yes, even better."

"All told, how many pieces of property have you owned in Seattle?"

"I'd say 55 or 56," Beck said.

"What was the cheapest?"

"That first lot I bought from Mr. Whitney—$500."

"And the most expensive?"

"I think the Sheridan Beach property. I paid $6,800 for two lots on the lake and sold them for $57,500; then I purchased three lots and built a house costing me approximately $70,000 (and later sold it for $160,000). Today it's worth $250,000."

"The asking price is $440,000," Pat said.

"Yes," Beck said, "But I don't think it's worth that."

"And then there was the Grosvenor House," Pat said.

"I went in with a group and bought it," Beck explained. "I put up $50,000 as my share, and I took a $240,000 profit out of it."

"I realize this is supposition," Pat said, "but because of your troubles with the IRS, with their attaching and liening all of your properties, what would you estimate they might have cost you?"

Beck didn't even pause to think about it. He had the figure on the tip of his tongue. "It has cost me at least $3-to-$5 million dollars," he said.

"Say, you had gone into real estate instead of the labor movement," Pat continued. "You would have earned a large fortune."

"Millions," Beck said, matter-of-factly. "I would have made millions. I'd have bought everything I could have put my hands on down in the Regrade District. I bought the property where the Teamsters are presently located; put $75,000 into it and could sell for a million tomorrow. I bought the TraveLodge for $90,000 and sold it for $430,000."

"You didn't sell the TraveLodge immediately," Pat said. "How much rent did you take out of that property?"

"I netted $45,000 a year," Beck said.

"For how many years?"

"Three. It built up to that from a starting point of about $15,000," Beck recalled.

"In other words," Pat said, "you got your original investment back, plus $430,000?"

"Yes."

"Then the $430,000 was net."

"Yes. Then I bought a piece of property on the corner of Thomas and Boren Avenue and put a building on it," Beck said. "My initial investment was about $145,000. The land cost me $25,000 and I borrowed $100,000 to build the building. Then I leased it out for 10 years to the Spaulding Sporting Goods Company. I got back every cent I ever put into it and then I sold it to the *Seattle Times* for $300,000."

"Dave, what was your motivation?" Pat asked. "Was it the money? Or was it more of a game to you, like chess?"

"It was both," Beck said. "After I'd been working for the union four or five years, my salary was $12,000 a year. That was good money for those times. Then when I started buying and selling my various properties, I made a practice of borrowing from the banks. At one time I owed Seattle-First National Bank $350,000 at 4% interest. One day I got a telephone call from Mr. Morgan at the bank. He said he wanted me to come down and talk to him. He told me that his superiors had advised him that the bank was increasing the interest rate ½ percent. I told Mr. Morgan I wouldn't pay it. 'You'll have to, you have a note coming due,' he said. I'd been paying 90-day commercial notes off regularly; sometimes $300 and $400 payments, other times $3,000 or $4,000 or $5,000, if I'd sold some property. But my balance at the time Mr. Morgan spoke to me was $350,000. So I asked him, 'How many days do I have?' Eighteen or 20 days, he said. 'All right,' I told him, 'I will see what I can do—but I am *not* going to pay that extra half percent.'

"Now, Art Morgenstern, an insurance man, was a friend of mine. We went through the Elks Lodge together when I was Exalted Ruler. I went to him and I said, 'Art, contact one of your insurance companies and find out if there's any chance of borrowing $350,000. I'll put up my properties for collateral.' He said he would phone around and see what he could do. Two days later he phoned me back. He asked, 'When are you going to be in Los Angeles?' I told him I was going down there the following Tuesday. He said he would meet me there. 'I have arranged for you to talk to some people about that real estate loan,' he said.

"Now, what I am going to tell you next probably sounds like a fairy tale, but it's the God's honest truth. On Tuesday, Art Morgenstern and I were just entering the new office building of the Occidental Insurance Company in L.A., when this fellow comes along and says, 'Hello, Dave.' Startled, I turned to him and asked, 'Do I know you?' He said, 'Oh, yes, you do.' I said, 'I don't think so. I'm afraid you've made a mistake.' 'Now, listen,' he said. 'You slept in a hammock right across from me in 1917 when we both were in boot training. It was at Balboa Park in the old California Building.' I said, 'By God, I *do* know you. What are you doing here?' And he said, 'What are *you* doing here?' I told him I was going upstairs to try and arrange for a loan. He asked me the name of the loan officer I was going to meet. 'Why?' I asked him. 'Because,' he said, 'I am the president of the Occidental Insurance Company. By God, Dave, I will sit in on the meeting with you.' Fifteen minutes later, Art and I walked out of the building with a promise from the company that it would approve the loan after first investigating my collateral. Their appraisers came to Seattle, estimated that my assets amounted to nearly $600,000, and I got the loan at 4 percent interest. I asked them to make the check payable to Seattle-First

National Bank, I turned it over to Mr. Morgan, and I paid Occidental off over the next 10 years at 4 percent. After that I never had any further problems financing my property purchases. Along the way, my union salary went from $12,000 a year, to $15,000, to $25,000 in 1947, and finally to $50,000 after my election as president in 1952.

"Now, take the International Union headquarters building in Washington, D.C. I personally picked the land it is sitting on. Nobody else had a thing to do with it. I bought it from the American Legion for $350,000. I went over and had a friend of mine get an option on it so that when the news broke that the Teamsters were interested in it, the price wouldn't skyrocket. We got a 60-day option. Dan Tobin screamed bloody murder. At first, he was against it, but he finally came around, and we bought the property. Then we put up the building for about another $5.5 million. The last estimate I heard was that the place is now worth $17,600,000. So, summing up, I'd say I did pretty well in real estate—both for the Teamsters and myself."

16
Money Talk

O<small>N THE</small> subject of his personal wealth, Dave Beck was quite guarded most of his adult life. He would neither confirm nor deny that he was an authentic millionaire; a half a million, maybe, but not a full-grown one. Anyway, inasmuch as he invested heavily, both for the Teamsters and himself, in the local area, the bankers of Seattle were happy to see him come—and so were a lot of other financiers.

Because of his reputation for reticence on personal money matters, it came as something of a surprise to hear him talk so candidly about finances (his) during a speaking engagement in 1978. There was nothing secretive about Dave Beck on that day. He was in great form, the Dave Beck of old—ranting, vociferous, animated, his voice reverberating with thunder and fervor. The occasion was a weekly Chamber of Commerce luncheon at Bellevue, in suburban Seattle, packed with local dignitaries, captains of industry, TV and newspaper reporters.

Sharing the head table with him, I asked Beck what his topic was going to be. "I don't know yet," he said. "By the time I get up there, I'll think of something. I'll *wing* it."

"Where are your notes?"

"Notes? I never use notes."

Only a couple of months shy of his 84th birthday, Beck was a model of supreme confidence as he stood before the audience. Starting out slowly, with a measured glint in his eye, he said he was flattered by the warm introduction given him.

"I'm reminded," he said, "of the speaker who was going around the United States giving talks. He came to this particular town, where it took the toastmaster 10 minutes to introduce him. When he finally got up to talk, the speaker turned to the toastmaster and said: 'That is the most wonderful introduction I've ever had. I wish I could say all the admirable things about you that you just said about me.' And the toastmaster replied: 'You could—if you were as big a liar as I am.'"

Students of Dave Beck have endeavored for years to capture in print the special quality, the rich tartness, the pure body and flavor of his oratory. They have seldom succeeded. The human ear is a wonderful instrument, but not so wonderful as the Beck larynx. The pencil of a stenographer may catch a phrase here and there and hold it, but something escapes in translation from notebook to type.

A cassette recorder is required for proper reproduction. The following is pure Beck, a transcription I made during his speech at Bellevue:

"Over the years, I have spoken before hundreds and hundreds and hundreds of chambers and clubs and labor unions all over the United States, down in Mexico, in South America. I've been a delegate to the British Trade Union Congress for the American Federation of Labor. I've spoken in London, Holland, France, Ireland, and many, many places. But I like to speak, primarily, to business people. . .employees and those in the high echelon of business. I like to represent myself as speaking largely in be-half of labor.

"I don't apologize one minute for what's occurred in the American labor movement in recent years, because it's a normal, natural evolution. I've spoken time after time after time and answered questions—when somebody would rise and ask, 'Mr. Beck, why all the fighting in these trade unions?' And I always remind them that the fighting, and the progress we have made, is not at all unusual—whether it's in the labor movement or any other part of our social and economic system. We must never forget that America was *born* in revolution. In 1775 we fought a revolutionary war with the British Empire to establish this government. And from that time on until around 1861, with revolutionary progress, we continued to grow and develop this country. We did not solve all its problems; we had continuity of trouble; we were in conflict constantly, between capital and labor and religion and black and white—all the pains of a new nation. But in the process we continued to make progress.

"I have been around the world—and over in Europe at least 27 times—down in South America and over in the Orient—and I can say without fear of contradiction that, sure we have trouble in our country. Labor's had trouble; capital's had trouble. The black man has had trouble; the Orientals have had trouble; and religions have had troubles. But there is no country in the world that can even start to compare with this government of ours.

"All through my life in the labor movement—and it started in 1914—and I was a member of the Teamsters International Union in a local capacity from '14 up to '26, and from 1926 up to 1958, when I reached the age of 63 and qualified for 30 years of continuous service and retired on a pension of $50,000 a year, as long as I live. Now, a lot of people say right away: '$50,000! Wow!' Granted, that's a good pension, but let's compare it with what I might have made if I hadn't dedicated my life to labor. Let's talk real estate investments, for example. I sold my interest in the Grosvenor House, the first big apartment house ever constructed in the Denny regrade area—one of my associates in that project was Charley Horowitz, now on the Supreme Court bench—I sold my share for a profit of over $260,000. I worked for the Teamsters International Union from 1952 to 1957 for total salary of $250,000. I sold a piece of property to the Northgate developers, just to the south of Northgate—I originally paid $14,000 for it and got $140,000 for it. I sold the TraveLodge, at Sixth and John, just a month ago, for $430,000—a profit of more than $300,000 over my original investment. I sold another piece of real estate, the Sunset Distributing Co. in Ballard, for $110,000 more than I paid for it. Back in Washington, D.C., when I was president of the Teamsters and was looking for a site on which to build our four-story, $5-million headquarters, I bought the property from the American Legion for $350,000. Today it's worth between $15 and $17 million. I also bought the property for the Teamsters' building here in Seattle; one block by a half-block, $60,000. Today it's valued at $400,000, just for the land alone.

"Recently, I got my pencil out and started playing around with some figures. I was curious to know how much money in salary I earned in all the years I was on the Teamsters' payroll. The total came to $684,000. A lot of money, sure, but, hell, I earned 12 times that for the Teamsters on the property deals I handled for them. Yet you never read about that in the papers when they write about Dave Beck. I believe in freedom of speech—I believe in the First Amendment—I believe in everything associated with a free country—and I have no objection when they attack me; but I'd like to be able to answer my critics occasionally."

Several weeks before Dave made this speech, he was back in the news:

Seattle—(AP)—Despite a plea from the federal government, former Teamster leader Dave Beck has been allowed five years to repay more than $700,000 in back taxes to the Internal Revenue Service.

The Justice Department filed a complaint seeking $846,000 in back taxes and seeking foreclosure on mortgages of Seattle property Beck owns or foreclosure of tax liens pending against him. King County Superior Court Judge Horton Smith rejected a government contention that they did not have jurisdiction in the case and said he had no cause to delay the matter.

Beck, 83, has argued successfully that he has made payments of about $600,000 in recent years to the IRS and will make the others, but to force sale of the property would mean considerable financial loss.

With stunning candor, Beck alluded to his tax problems during the Bellevue address.

"The other day," Beck continued, "*Argus*, the Seattle weekly, asked on its front page: 'Why does Beck fight? Why doesn't he just sit back and enjoy himself in peace?' I can tell you in a very short minute why Beck continues to fight the IRS. I have nothing against the IRS personally. I fight them in the courts, because I have a *right* to fight them there. Now, let's take just one piece of property, as an example. Let's take the TraveLodge at Sixth and John in Seattle. Some real estate dealers brought in an offer of $175,000. When that was tossed out of court, another offer was made for $200,000; again, no go. Then they turned around and approved the sale of it for $225,000; finally, $250,000. And it was sold, as I said before, for $430,000.

"To put the facts of my battle with the IRS in proper perspective, it is necessary to go back six years. At that time I entered into an agreement as the Dorothy Beck Estate with the IRS to pay off back taxes over a period of five years and then negotiate the balance of any remaining amount. For four years that agreement was met. Approximately $680,000 in cash was paid the government. Then, during the fifth year, it became impossible to carry out the terms of the agreement. A mortgage was placed on one of my properties, and it became necessary to sell one of my personal properties to raise $200,000 in order to make the IRS payment. My second wife was suffering from terminal cancer, and her medical bills were running high. She died in April of 1977. Her care prevented me from looking after my business.

"Her condition was noted in the newspapers. Surely the IRS knew about it, yet four months before she passed away and without first notifying me, the IRS moved to place a lien against my $50,000 pension from the Teamsters. This was accomplished through the Teamsters' International office in Washington, D.C. My attorneys knew nothing of this action until after it had been filed.

"That was in December, and in January the IRS started grabbing my monthly pension check, $4,166.66. In February, same thing. In March, they were nice to me; they kept only $3,948.99 and let me keep $217.67. After that I got to keep $217.67 a month. It's still going on. My attorney tells me the IRS action is *inhuman*. I finally had to borrow huge sums to pay off the medical bills. My appeal to the IRS to reconsider the facts fell on deaf ears.

"Four times the IRS, through its regional division, took me to court, trying to force me to sell some of my properties at prices *below* my figures. They wanted me to sell the TraveLodge for $250,000, but I vigorously asked for $400,000—in fact, one prospective purchaser offered $430,000. In the last several months I have sold properties that will allow me to pay the IRS about $670,000. That'll bring the total I have paid the IRS from my late wife's estate to about $1,354,000 over the last six years. About $600,000 of that was interest! Of the total amount owed, a half-million of it dates back to 1941.

"But enough about my tax fight . . . .

"Why does anyone join a labor union? There's only one reason. We can't all be doctors, dentists, lawyers, professors, or professional people. Some of us must follow the other phases of the master work plan. We join labor unions for protection. Most workers, 98 percent of them, don't own any real estate, merchandise, mill, mine, or factory, no farms—they own only one thing: their *labor*. And they sell that labor in the open marketplace for the best price they can get under our system of free enterprise. That's the only reason they organize.

"Now, just because someone happens to be the greatest doctor in the United States doesn't mean that he can come in and head up a great labor organization. And a great union leader certainly couldn't go in and become a great doctor. You can carry that back and forth. But what worries me as I look down the road into the future—and I've been through many a recession, a depression, label it what you will—is whether or not we can keep finding solutions to our problems of economics. I remember the day when labor went out on strike, strike breakers came from clear across the U.S. I saw it on the Seattle waterfront, 35 or 40 years ago, when they built a fence down the whole waterfront—and brought men from the Gulf to break that strike. Today you can't bring *anybody* across state lines to break a strike. So in that phase of political action we have gained.

"For years, I have advocated 100 percent opposition to labor becoming a political party. I have never believed in it. Yes, labor has to protect its interest, in the city, or the county, or the village, or the state legislature, or the Congress; it has to do it, but it must be done by economic action, not political.

"I attended my first meeting of the Teamsters international convention in 1925 in Seattle. We had a national membership then of 78,000. I then put in the Western Conference of Teamsters physical structure and changed the whole organizing pattern of America. It has since been adopted by practically every international union. We have gone from 78,000 members in 1925 to more than 2,000,000. I turned the Teamsters over to Jimmy Hoffa in 1957 with a national membership of 1,580,000 people. Yes, the Teamsters have grown. I put into the pockets of the men I spoke for in the United States and Canada hundreds of millions of dollars; increased wages, shorter hours at higher pay, better working conditions, and other important gains.

"In the old days, if you ran into a strike, there was no place to turn. And when it came to settling inflation or deflation, you settled it out there in the open city. You could last five weeks, 10 weeks, 20 weeks. Now what's happening? After a short spell, unless you're a direct party to a strike, you can go down and sign up for unemployment insurance. You're on health and welfare; you're on all those things in which tremendous gains have been made, aside from wages, hours, and conditions of employment. Sure, it has changed the pattern of our lives; all for the better, too.

"You hear a lot today about the misappropriation of union funds. Do you know that Jimmy Hoffa or any member of the labor group in the central and southern states never invested one dollar in Las Vegas, Reno, or any hotel corporation except after the six employer board members agreed to do so? And yet, you've never heard one of those employers named in the press or on TV. But six of them voted along with Hoffa and five others on every single loan made. Now, I'm not in accord with that loan policy adopted by the central and southern states. I want to make it clear that, in a large measure, the Teamsters International is patterned after the federal government. The Teamsters, therefore, cannot control the finances of the local union, or of the Joint Council, or of the Western Conference. There's no democratic process if they could. They have a right to invest their own money.

"Let's take a look at the Western Conference of Teamsters. Can you give me one instance—did you ever read of one, did you ever hear of one—where anyone invested a single dollar of Western Conference funds that wasn't accounted for? *Anywhere?* One single dollar that wasn't accounted for 100 percent? You cannot do so, because it just never happened. As late as summer 1978 the *Wall Street Journal* and the national press carried front-page articles affirming everything I have claimed. Every dollar we invested went through insurance companies for health and welfare and such. Every dollar of it went to banks for investment. Right now, up in Alaska, every dollar invested by the Teamsters up there goes through banks. That's a necessity, in my opinion. But you'll have to change certain programs and certain constitutional procedure to bring compulsion to it.

"Personally, I have no objection to investigation, except that it causes a problem: it encourages some people to come in and play politics with such an investigation. I welcomed an investigation of the Western Conference of Teamsters. I had nothing to hide. Not a single, solitary dollar of Teamster money in the 11 western states has ever been invested without the most careful attention to sound business judgment. Take Bellevue here. When it was in swaddling clothes, when it was just getting started, Bell & Valdez built one of the first big housing developments in the area. Well, Metropolitan Life took one side of that project and I, in behalf of the Teamsters, took the other half. Together, we put several millions into it. Once, I took out of the banks in Indianapolis over $8 million and in one day brought it here to Seattle and put it in local banks—in one day. Over the years, as general president, I invested millions and millions of Teamsters' dollars, and, to the best of my knowledge, I never lost a penny of it. And I never lost a penny of my own, either.

"People ask me about communism. Back in the 1930s, communism tried to take over the labor movement. I didn't want communism. I fought it inside the trades union movement ever since I joined. I remember once sharing the podium with Prime Minister Attlee of Great Britain. I had just come up from a private meeting with Sir Winston Churchill in London at 10 Downing Street, and now Attlee and I were about to address the British Trades Union Congress. When it came my turn to speak, the commies cut all the wires in the place. So I went out on the boardwalk and made a 20-minute extemporaneous speech that was carried all over England and back to the States. I had no time for communism—I've *never* had any time for it.

"I have said it time and time again, the greatest gov-

ernment in the world, not only in its fundamental constitutional structure, but in its program revolving around
its investment in industry, labor, and everything else,
remains the United States. *We have the finest government in the world.* Sure, we make mistakes. But those mistakes can be reduced to a minimum. And you're not going
to solve your problems by hearing only one side of the
story.

"I earlier recited to you my experiences with the IRS.
To sum up, I defy anyone from the IRS to refute *one* of
those statements. They *cannot* do it, because it's the truth.
No doubt a lot of you have listened to the gossip that Dave
Beck was convicted of income tax evasion. That's false. I
never was convicted of evasion of taxes in my life; that is,
convictions that stuck. I beat Judge Boldt's decision in the
appellate court in San Francisco on every single charge. I
have had four libel cases, and I won them all. Sure, I have
had to fight all my life, but I *enjoy* it. I really do, I like a
good fight. Let me tell you, when you're fighting the IRS
it's a fight to the finish. It's bare-knuckle time. If I've spent
a dollar in defense of myself against them, I've spent a
million and a half. That's a lot of money, a million and a
half. And I'm not broke yet, I'm still doing all right. I'm
borrowing a little bit—I've tested the friendship of some of
my good friends—but I've got the settlement down to
about $300,000, if I paid the IRS off tomorrow. And if I
gave them the money tomorrow, by selling off a piece of my
property, I'd still be up there around a million. So at 83
years of age, no one is going to have to toss a benefit for old
Dave Beck.

"So now I have come to the end of my little recital. It
is time for questions. Ask me anything you want, regardless of my privacy, and I will answer you honestly. I have
nothing to hide. My first wife died after 43 years of
marriage; my second died after 10 years. So I have a good
batting record there and fear no questions in that direction. Fire away."

A young lawyer was the first to raise his hand.

"Mr. Beck, what was the toughest thing you ever did in organizing a union?"

"The toughest?"

"Yes."

Beck rubbed his chin, reflectively.

"They were *all* tough. I don't know, I've organized some of the greatest employers in America. You're probably too young to remember, but the older members of the chamber here no doubt remember the Second World War when they carried old Sewell Avery out of Montgomery Ward in Chicago because he wouldn't deal with the union. Well, I went in there and, with the Chicago people, organized that big department store. Then we bought several million dollars worth of Montgomery Ward stock at a time when a big investor named Wolfstone was trying to take over as a majority stockholder. So when some of the union chiefs telephoned me from Detroit and asked me who to vote for in the battle for control, I said Avery and the management. That's the way they voted, Avery and the management won, and Mr. Avery and I became warm friends. When it came time to sign the contract, he insisted that I represent the Teamsters International. I said, 'Who's going to sign for Montgomery Ward?' He replied, 'My assistant.' And I said, 'Jimmy Hoffa, from Detroit, will be signing for us.' And Mr. Avery said, 'Oh, no he won't. I'll sign and you'll sign.' Which we did. That was a tough one."

Another hand flew up.

"Mr. Beck, in your opinion, what happened to Jimmy Hoffa?"

"I think he was murdered. There's no doubt about it. But *why* it happened, I don't know. Jimmy, of course, had been talking or making threats to people that he perhaps had commitments to in the field of investments—they figured he was going to talk—and if he did, it would cause them a lot of embarrassment and grief. So they got rid of him.

"I'll tell you about Jimmy Hoffa. In 1952 several months before the Teamsters convention, I kept Hoffa off of our general executive board. I refused to vote for him on the basis that the West had made such tremendous progress and was entitled to the existing vacancy. President Dan Tobin insisted that the vote be unanimous. I told him he'd never get it, because I'd not vote for anyone except a westerner. And a westerner was elected. Hoffa was not elected until the convention of the following October when the board was increased by two more seats.

"Now, socially, I never was close to Hoffa, even though he worked under my direction as a vice-president for a couple of years. But he was an amazing organizer, they'll never cheat him out of that—one of the greatest organizers in the history of the trades union movement, and I've met them all. John L. Lewis, Bill Green, you name them; Hoffa was topnotch in that respect. Where Jimmy went astray—*if* he did go astray—was his choice of associates in his later years. Some of them were of questionable character."

"Mr. Beck, what is the story behind your successful organizing of Los Angeles, years ago?"

"I remember," Beck said, "when I was dealing with the Casey brothers. They were the original owners of the United Parcel Service in Seattle. They started right down here at Pioneer Square. If you go down there and look carefully, you'll see their initials chiseled in the sidewalk where they started. Now, we organized UPS in Seattle, Tacoma, Portland, and on down the coast to San Francisco-Oakland. But when it came time to go into Los Angeles, we hit a brick wall. I mean, we couldn't make a dent. So I went to Mike Casey, head of the Teamsters in San Francisco, a very able fellow, and my superior officer at the time, and I said to him, 'What's the matter, Mike? Why can't we break into L.A.? We're even getting the cold shoulder from United Parcel Service there. Why is it we can work for UPS in other cities—under union shops, ideal conditions, never any strikes—and we can't work for them in L.A.?'

"Mike said, 'Dave, the UPS office there told me if they

ever get into position, they'd like to do business with us, but the Merchants and Manufacturers Association, the L.A. Chamber of Commerce, and the Industrial Association will be adverse to UPS signing a contract with the Teamsters.'

"So I called Jim Casey at UPS for a conference on the subject and I said, 'Well, where does that leave us?' And he shook his head, and said, 'I don't know, you figure it out.' I said, 'That's exactly what I'm going to do.' So I told the Caseys, 'You go back and tell your associates that, starting on the termination of the first contract presently in existence on the West Coast, from Vancouver, B.C., all the way down to Bakersfield, California, we will carry out our contracts to the letter. I have never broken a contract in my life. But when that contract terminates, we are either going to work for UPS in Los Angeles on the same labor conditions as in other cities or we are *not* going to work for you in any other city.'

"This procedure of organizing was followed through every industry in Southern California.

"So Casey went back to the Los Angeles Industrial Association and notified them of what I said. He asked them, 'What am I going to do?' They told him, 'Don't worry. No matter what it costs—a million, two million, *five* million—we will underwrite your fight with the Teamsters in Los Angeles.' And Casey said, 'Will you also underwrite the same fight in Sacramento, and Oakland, and San Francisco, and Portland and Seattle, et cetera?' And they said, 'No! But we'll underwrite it at Los Angeles.' 'Well,' Casey told them, 'if I have to fight the Teamsters in the western part of the United States, and later on maybe all over the country, I'll have to sign with the Teamsters and take my chances with you here in L.A.' And from that day to this, we've been organized with United Parcel Service in Los Angeles with no interruptions or labor disturbances of any significance. Soon after, we did identically the same thing with all the other major companies there.

"When we first went into Los Angeles, in 1935, we had 315 members working in the movie studios. We came out of

L.A. with over 100,000 members organized, and today the Los Angeles Joint Council is either first or second in membership of any joint council affiliated with the Teamsters and that includes New York and Chicago. That's progress."

End of speech.

17

Old Warriors Never Die

DAVE Beck and I were sitting in his apartment talking about an article which appeared in the morning paper. The writer had speculated on the disappearance of Jimmy Hoffa 15 months before just after Hoffa started a drive to reclaim the presidency of the Teamsters from those he had put in charge when he went to prison in 1967. The general executive board by unanimous action named Fitzsimmons.

"With the vanished Hoffa," stated the article, "went the secrets he had threatened to spill to the authorities about underworld influence in the union that exercises stop-or-go power over a million trucks."

In the same newspaper was a column by Jack Anderson, beginning: "Federal investigators are quietly tightening the vise on the tumultuous Teamsters Union, which, they claim, is the most corrupt in the country. The FBI and Labor Department have joined forces to crack down on the alleged corruption. Their investigation isn't aimed at the rank-and-file truck drivers, a rugged but solid breed, who are known for their square dealing. The targets are a few free-wheeling Teamsters leaders who allegedly have chiseled the drivers out of union money."

Beck put the paper down. I was still trying to return to the original concept of the book, and my plan was to spend the morning talking to him about anything he wanted to get off his chest. I had a clipboard ready with some questions on it. Those newspaper articles seemed like a good place to start.

"Was the union clean of mob influences when you were president?" I asked.

"As far as I could tell," Beck said.

"How could you be sure?"

"Listen," he said. "In all the years I was in the trades union movement, I'd take a solemn oath that never in my life could I honestly say I knew of one person in the Teamsters who was directly or indirectly in the mob. I don't think the mobsters wanted any part of the trades union movement. Their business was narcotics, gambling, prostitution, and pornography. I'm not saying they didn't have trucks or drivers in our union—I don't honestly know—but if they did, I never knew it. They'd never keep you advised of anything they owned. When I say 'The Mob', I'm not talking about a lot of hoodlums in Los Angeles or Chicago or Detroit or St. Louis or New York; I'm talking about the actual Mob—the Mafia. I think the Mafia is a tightly-knit organization that is harder to crack and become a member of than it is to be President of the United States. I suppose I must have met some of the Mafia somewhere down the road, but I don't know who they were."

"Johnny Dio, the New York freelance entrepreneur and business investor, did he once offer to put up $20,000 of his own money to start a Teamsters' local?"

"No, not to my knowledge. He made no offers to me. I never had any business relations with him of any kind or character. My right-hand man in New York was Tom Hickey, one of our vice-presidents. I had a lot of confidence in Tom. He was a good man. So when Jimmy Hoffa came to me and recommended that the International authorize a charter sponsored by Dio, I turned him down. I told Hoffa, 'The taxicab charter is going to someone in whom I have unquestionable faith. He must be honest, he must have integrity. That man is Hickey. As for Dio, he will never get a Teamsters taxicab charter as long as I'm president because he is not identified with labor. He is strictly a businessman. (He never did, either.) I said to Hoffa, 'Hickey is handling New York, he'll continue handling New York.'

"What happened," continued Beck, "was that I sent Einar Mohn, Larry Steinberg, and Buddy Graham to New York to look over the situation, and then come back to me and report. They came back and said it was clearly a decision for the Joint Council of New York to make. In granting a new charter, the routine is that it has to go first before the Joint Council, which okays or rejects it. Once they approve a recommendation, it is then sent into the National Office, where the final determination is made either by the general president or the board. In the case of the New York taxicab charter, Mohn and Steinberg came back and said the Joint Council approved the nomination of Tom Hickey, and that ended the debate. I passed the recommendation along to our board, it was okayed, and Tom got the charter. Dio was out. I liked that. Hickey was my friend then, he was my friend years after, and he was still my friend when he died."

Where mobsters were concerned, Beck was adamant. Never in his labor career, he testified, did he ever hire a known member of the underworld.

"Most of that Mafia talk is baloney," he said. "I never *carried* a handgun in my life (though we once stationed some guards in our Seattle building to protect ourselves during the jurisdictional and other fights of the 1930s). Nor did I ever take a personal bodyguard along on my travels. But if you go down to the *Seattle P-I* and check the 1950 files, sometime in there, you will find these headlines: 'DAVE

BECK'S SON THREATENED WITH KIDNAPPING.' I never knew anything about it until I got a phone call from the FBI. I was told that the G-Men were looking for Dave, Jr.; they were concerned about his safety. I wanted details. They said it was too risky to discuss them over the phone. But the facts were these: FBI agents had just learned that a pair of parolees from Leavenworth Penitentiary were on their way to Seattle to kidnap my son. Well, we found Dave. Jr., within a half-hour, we hired a bodyguard, and gave him around-the-clock protection. Next day the FBI phoned me back. They had picked up two suspects and wanted me to come right over and identify them. I was escorted into this little room, with a small window of one-way glass, where I could eye the suspects but they couldn't see me. Well, I didn't know either of them. I went back to my office and thumbed through all our records. I discovered that one of the men had once been a member of the cab drivers' union.

"I had to ask myself, how did the FBI pick up the tip that the parolees intended to snatch Dave, Jr.? I guessed it must have come from inside Leavenworth. The suspects probably shot off their mouths before getting out, bragging how they would kidnap 'millionaire' Beck's boy and collect a big ransom. In my opinion, the tip came from an FBI plant. No? Then why did it take the government so long to prosecute the suspects? The FBI didn't want to blow its cover at the prison. Buy my theory or not, it was a strange experience for the Becks. This is all part of FBI records and newspaper files."

"Your retirement," I said, "left the presidency open. Some of the news magazines speculated that you would throw your support behind Frank Brewster against Hoffa."

Beck shook his head vigorously.

"No, no, no," he protested. "I never made any such expression. Why, to the best of my knowledge, Brewster never even said anything about opposing Hoffa. The only two candidates of any prominence were Bill Lee and Jimmy."

"Brewster never even had a preliminary discussion with you about running?" I asked.

"No."

"What happened to him in the race for vice-president?" I wanted to know.

"When Frank came up for re-election, his opponents ran George Mock of Sacramento against him, and after counting 100 or so of local delegates' votes, Brewster withdrew," Beck said. All of this is a matter of convention proceedings, well documented in the Teamsters published records.

"Did Brewster remain head of the Western Conference?"

"No. After Hoffa was elected, he immediately removed Frank from office and replaced him with Einar Mohn."

"What is Brewster doing today?"

"He's retired," Beck said. "He's about 82, two years younger than me. Frank and I have been and continue to be friends. He was a great asset to me throughout my career in 'labor' for more than 50 years."

"Dave, I asked, "what was your impression of Hoffa the first time you met him?"

"Jimmy never made any particular impression on me," Beck replied. "He had the sort of personality that grew on you gradually. As I got to know him, I could sense that he had a hell of an ability as an organizer. And as you know, organizing is close to my heart. Hoffa first appeared on the labor scene in 1933 or '34. No, I couldn't picture him as a future president. Before I told him I was retiring, he came to me many times and said, 'Now, Dave, if you run for re-election, you have my support.'"

Twenty-one years afterward, probably the sharpest memory the public has of Beck is of his appearance on TV before the Senate committee hearings. They have not forgotten the fierce language Chairman John McClellan used to tongue-lash Beck. He flaunted such phrases as "flagrant disrespect for honest unionism," and "arrogant contempt for honest laboring Teamsters," and he questioned Beck's right to borrow money from the Teamsters' union treasury.

"The question frequently comes up as to whether or not I was treated fairly by the committee," Beck said. "No, I was not, because I don't think a Senate investigation body ever gives a witness fair treatment. Your attorney, for example, cannot subject the committee members to cross-examination. They used some pretty strong language and I couldn't even sue for libel. In a real court trial, where I had the right of cross-examination and where the rules of evidence applied, I would have come out of the hearings clean and white 100 percent.

"Because there was no cross-examination on our part, I *had* to take the Fifth Amendment, if I was going to protect myself against other legal procedures pending in court. You must remember, the federal government was still investigating those income tax cases against me. Now, McClellan and his committee were attempting to ask me questions along these lines. Had I replied, my attorney had no opportunity to cross-examine the committee members, such as Bobby Kennedy, who represented the attorney general's office. The only way I was able to protect myself against future appearances in a federal court, without a prejudicial position having been established against me, was to exercise the Fifth Amendment. This was on the instructions of Edward Bennett Williams, one of the greatest lawyers in America. I carried out his instructions by refusing to respond to questions and thus exercising my constitutional right guaranteed by the Fifth Amendment. Mr. Williams did caution me, however, to handle myself with courtesy in front of the committee, and the most courteous way to avoid any dispute was to take the Fifth. I think I kept my poise. I remained quite calm, even when Bobby Kennedy tried to bait me. Some of his questions were just plain nasty. I would have loved facing Bobby on neutral grounds. I'd have given him some of his own medicine. Absolutely.

"Before going into the hearing room, my attorney told me, 'We are not going in here and answer questions where we have no right to cross-examinations.' George Meany, incidentally, was supporting the position of Bobby Kennedy and Senator McClellan. So when I kept taking the Fifth Amendment, I was only exercising my rights. Many Americans have been led down the blind path by being told that taking the Fifth is contrary to good citizenship. I don't agree. It is a part of our Constitution; it is written in there for a citizen's protection. A person is innocent of anything until proven guilty by a jury of his peers. He has no such right where he is deprived of cross-examination. The proof of all this is that when we did have the right to cross-examine and the right of appeal, we won in every single case. Go check the record.

"I don't know what actuated Meany to come to the conclusion that he was going to stake everything on what finally led up to the expulsion of the Teamsters from the A.F.ofL. What binding association that existed between Meany and Senator John Kennedy, brother Bobby and McClellan, and the rest, I don't know. Generally, though, John Kennedy was not very vocal during the hearings, except to ask me several routine questions. The rest of the time he just sat back and listened.

"In order to use the Fifth Amendment, I could not answer a single question. If I had, then I would have had to answer everything. So if you go back and get the transcript of what Bobby Kennedy asked me, it went along these lines: 'Do you know your mother?' And if I had said yes, I would have been answering a question, and then I would have had to answer any question asked. Somebody figured it out; they said I took the Fifth Amendment 142 times in the two days I faced the committee. That sounds about right."

"Do you believe there was a conspiracy to make an example of you?" I asked.

"That was probably part of it," Beck said. "Right from the very first day I started moving up in the labor movement, I recognized it was going to be a dogfight. I had to accept the fact that my enemies would be trying to beat me with everything they could cook up. They'd play under the table and over the table and in the corners and down in the basement; they'd accuse me of everything in the world. They would go to any length to destroy me. Management, other unions, independent truckers, ambitious people within your own union; they were all part of it. Bad publicity was part of the game, too. My salvation was to ignore it, not let it get under my skin. I rode with the punches, but sooner or later I'd get to dish it out—and then my adversaries wished they'd never started it. The politics, the infighting, the dirty tricks all went with the lease. The Bobby Kennedys in my life never made that much difference. But I knew they would do everything they could to crucify me if they could get away with it. And I was going to pay them back any way I could to hold my ground. And I did—and I still am.

"When Bobby Kennedy was investigating me, an IRS agent named Watson, admitted under cross-examination on the witness stand that he'd started out in Seattle and traveled across the United States into virtually every city of 15,000 population and over. When he got to Chicago, for example, he'd go to the IRS office there, and they'd supply him with a staff crew, from five to 25 people. Then they'd visit every bank in town, trying to find private safe deposit boxes belonging to Dave Beck. They found nothing. It must have cost the federal government, without prosecution costs, at least $15 million. I estimate that those trials cost me, personally, a million and a half. Luckily, I was in a position where I could make money in real estate and business investments. In the first six months of the trial, all the salary I had ever earned from the Teamsters, $684,000 from 1926 to 1957, flew out the window—all of it! That didn't concern me. But there was our government, pouring millions into the case, and for what? They finally wound up losing every income tax charge against me. All that money wasted, right down the sewer."

As an outgrowth of the Senate investigation, the Executive Council of the American Federation of Labor-

Congress of Industrial Organizations ousted Beck as a vice-president and as a member of the council. He had refused to appear before the council, organized labor's highest tribunal in those days, to answer charges of corruption within the Teamsters. George Meany and his fellow union chiefs found Beck guilty of "gross misuse of union funds entrusted to his care." In 1957, the A.F.L.-C.I.O. expelled the Teamsters.

"The Senate rackets committee demonstrated repeatedly it was anti-Teamsters," Beck said. "Any report it issued was bound to be distorted, biased, and unfair. While one arm of the government was accusing me of thievery, another was trying to prove that the money was income on which I failed to pay taxes. That made about as much sense as most of the things the committee had to say. They said I brought shame on the American labor movement. They said I was motivated by an uncontrollable greed. They said I was miserly. And they claimed that our union was faced with a financial loss because of the way I managed Teamster funds. Hell, the Teamsters were in marvelous financial position at the time, and are now, both as to net assets and liquidity. Certainly we couldn't possibly have been in bad shape when we had several million dollars drawing higher interest rates than we would have paid for borrowing. Why, when I left office as president, the union had $14 million more in assets than when I went in—and nearly a half-million more members. I must have done something right."

"Let's talk about the presidency," I said. "Down the years, a lot of controversy has surrounded the Teamsters' No. 1 position. What were your qualifications?"

"I had the credentials," he answered. "Of course, my greatest qualification was my membership in the union from 1914 to 1952. Nearly 40 years of training on the job as business agent, secretary, vice-president, executive vice-president, and a close association with every phase of Teamster and employer relationships. In my opinion, I was thoroughly qualified in every respect."

"Even though you didn't have a formal education, a college degree?"

"Listen," Beck said, "a college education wasn't a necessity in those days nor now for that matter. Why, we've had Presidents of the United States who didn't have degrees, and we have had many outstanding businessmen without them. Pardon me if this sounds narrow-minded, but except for special instances like a doctor or a dentist or the law and engineering, where you must pass qualifying examinations, I honestly don't feel that a college degree is all that big an asset. Times without number I have personally seen, say, a businessman bring in an attorney to represent him in labor negotiations, and the secretary of the labor union would be sitting there doing his own negotiating. In the majority of cases the secretary was a guy who had been raised in the ghetto, yet he was far more qualified to handle the contract talks. That's why the employer brought in an attorney, because he, himself, never had enough confidence in himself to conduct those negotiations."

I said, "Tell me about your campaign in 1952 to replace Dan Tobin as president."

Beck laughed.

"I had no campaign," he said. "Tobin simply felt I was the best qualified and he nominated me. There were no other candidates. So I was elected."

"You said that the Teamsters pattern themselves after the federal government," I said. "That doesn't sound very democratic to me. Why were there no other candidates?"

"Granted, there were plenty of qualified men," Beck said. "But they obviously figured they couldn't beat me, so they refused to allow their names to go up for election. I think the fact that President Tobin was held in such high esteem by the Teamsters' general convention membership was what swung the election to me. When he got up on the floor and nominated me, that cinched it. Anybody could have been nominated, same as I, but I was the frontrunner.

I was well known and had been executive vice-president for the past five years."

"Did Tobin give any indication that he was grooming you to take his place? Surely, he must have said something to you."

"In the early summer of '52, shortly before the convention, Dan called me to his vacation place at Cape Cod, outside Boston, and told me he was retiring. I tried to talk him out of it. I said, Dan, don't quit, because I was doing most of his heavy organizing work out in the field. No, he said, he had already made up his mind. Whether his doctor had advised him to get out, I don't know. I know his health figured in his decision some way, because he died three years afterward. I think his physician told him that his life was limited and without telling anyone, not even me, he just simply decided to retire. Dan was well aware of my position. I had been stating for years that I would never be a candidate in an election opposing him; that if ever I did run, he'd have to personally nominate me. He did, I ran, and I won."

"Privately, it must have meant a lot to you to be head of the most powerful union in the world," I said.

"Not at all," Beck said. "The proof of that is I tried to talk Tobin into staying. For me, taking his place was just one more step up the ladder. It was not all that new to me. As leader of the national organization structure for about 10 years, I had been close to the presidency and was familiar with the duties of the office. So I really considered it a routine step as far as my working relationship with the International Union was concerned; from executive vice-president, a job especially created in the constitution for me, to president. The only big change in my private life was that I now had to spend more time in the East. I arranged for living quarters in Washington, D.C., whereas Tobin had preferred Indianapolis. For years I pestered Tobin to relocate in Washington, to build a headquarters there. So the first thing I did after my election was to begin construction of a new headquarters building. But I flew home to Seattle on weekends. I must have been the busiest commuter in the country."

"*Newsweek* once plastered it all over its cover that you had the power to bring all the wheels of America to a screeching halt," I said. "That was back in the mid-1950s. Do you think you were truly that powerful?"

Beck laughed again. His roar shook the room.

"Of course not," he said. "No individual in America, including the President of the United States, has that sort of power. No way was I influential enough to stop all of industry. Hell, the newspapers never credited me with that kind of power; they knew better. But it made a great magazine cover. It was just a figment of a misled editor's imagination. Sure, I could have slowed down industry a bit by going through constitutional procedure provided by the contracts we had with various companies; but bring the wheels of the U.S. to a total stop? Hell, I would have been hauled into court in a flash.

"I didn't even have the authority to call a nationwide Teamsters' strike. We had no control over anyone other than our own membership, and there were thousands of signed contracts between ourselves and individual industries that had to be honored. We couldn't interfere with those contracts without going through the wringer in court, resulting in horrendous damages against us. Teamsters have millions of dollars in their treasury, and they are certainly not going to open that up to litigation and damage suits they are almost certain to lose. No way. The only place I ever heard of it being tried was in the general strike in Seattle in 1919, and the Teamsters voted it down. Later, down in the Bay Area, in Oakland or San Francisco, some of the crafts unions tried it. When the Teamsters began to rumble, I went right in there and threatened to take away their charters if they didn't quiet down. That stopped it, right there."

"I heard a couple of rank-and-file Teamsters talking the other day," I said. "Your name came up; they were

members of the union when you were president. One of
them said he wished Dave Beck had never retired."

"I've heard those stories, too," Beck said. "But let's be
honest about it. While I still have the qualifications—while I still think as sharply as I ever did—my age is
against me. I'm 84. Under no conditions would I be a candidate again. Not for a second would I even think about it."

"And Hoffa?" I asked.

"If you're asking, was Jimmy qualified to take over the
reins again, the answer is unequivocally, yes," Beck said.
"But that wasn't the only issue involved. The question had
nothing to do with Hoffa's qualifications. The big issue was
whether the Teamsters' General Executive Board had
agreed to permit Hoffa to run for president again, in the
event Frank Fitzsimmons retired. Hoffa said yes, Fitz said
no. I'll take Fitz' word for it."

"You said the Teamsters pattern themselves after the
federal government," I said. "Well, a President of the
United States is limited to two terms of office now. How
does that compare with the Teamsters' presidency?"

"A president of the Teamsters may stand for re-election
as many times as the membership feels he is qualified
to serve," Beck explained. "Every five years he must face
another election; every five years the rank and file have a
right to keep him or kick him out. Delegates are chosen by
the locals and sent to convention, where the elections are
held. The rank and file are represented by their delegates.
Some unions hold direct elections by membership, the
Teamsters do not. I don't think, if we went to a direct
system, that it would change the outcome of our elections
much; it would be no more beneficial. I believe that our
voting system has provided us with competent leadership."

"If you were still president today, would you change
your tactics much?" I asked.

"Yes, certainly. I would be forced to keep abreast of
the times," he said. "Indeed, I couldn't do the same things
I did when I was an organizer. Labor was a lot rougher
then. Take the secondary boycott, as an example. Attor-

neys all over the U.S. are getting rich on the advocacy of legal tactics to get around the secondary boycott. I'll make a prophecy right now. If those Fancy Dan lawyers don't change, labor is going to refuse to sign long-term contracts. 'No more two-year agreements; no more three-year contracts,' they're going to say. 'No more five-year pacts. We will sign only an agreement for six months.' Then, under normal conditions, percentage in itself will see to it that an agreement lasts only *three* months, no matter what the issue may be. And then they go to business and say, 'Wait a minute here. You say this is not a labor issue. Well, we're asking you now for a greater increase in wages, shorter hours, and better working conditions. Kick that around for a while and then tell me it's not a labor issue. Let's see, then, if you can make your secondary boycott focus on that issue.' That's what is going to happen, and when it does, we're going to have the goddamndest industrial revolution this country has ever seen."

"Inevitably, there's the question of the black man's role in the labor movement," I said. "Take the South. When are they going to organize the southern states?"

"They *are* organizing," Beck pointed out. "The Teamsters are pretty well organized down there. The membership is not comparable to what it should be, but I'd say it is probably 100,000. That's a wild guess."

"Why have unions been so slow to move in the South? What's holding them up?" I asked.

"Why is it you only had slavery in the South?" Beck said. "In my opinion, that very situation will finally lead to the one-hundred percent unionization of the South. I know exactly what I would do if I were handling it. I'd concentrate on improving the conditions of black labor in the South. I think the strength of organizing black labor in the South is to solicit the support of black labor in the North. Well, you ask, if you organize the blacks, wouldn't that, in a sense, amount to reverse discrimination against whites?

Not in the South, it wouldn't. I can remember when I was driving a laundry truck. I had black laundry drivers working right alongside of me. There was no deep-rooted discrimination in Seattle.

"On the whole, the sore spot for the South in industry remains the black. It used to be that it wasn't even news when a lynching took place down there. But now you've got the black with a recognition of his rights alongside of the white man's, to the point where the black has developed strength enough to demand: 'Hey, wait a minute. Now, you just lynch one more brother down South—next week, the week after, or a month from now—and we're going to get the first eight whites who come into Harlem. *And we're going to lynch them!*

"Let us look at another phase of black and white employment. For an example, in organized baseball, for over 100 years there were no blacks employed in the sport at all. Now it is all equalized. The same can be said of many other instances, for this reason we are emphasizing the organization of blacks to give the black man a chance to catch up in drawing upon the benefits of better pay, hours, and working conditions of organized labor, where he has been deprived of equal opportunity for many, many years. This is not to in any way infer that we have any diminished interest in continuing to aggressively organize whites in the South as well, and everywhere else. I am simply trying to update and give consideration—recognizing that they have not had equal opportunity for over 100 years—and stop that discrimination right now. The great mass of the black people are not in business. They are earning their living in the fields of labor. Therefore, labor must assume a responsibility for equal opportunity of employment across the whole field of organized labor. The importance of this will be more fully recognized daily.

"In my opinion, the key to organizing the South is the Teamsters, working in conjunction with the black population in the North and supporting action from all other trades unions. Together, they can straighten out the problem down there."

"I was surprised to hear you say, once, that strikes should be avoided whenever possible," I said. "I mean, with your reputation as a militant and all."

"I've been saying that for 40 years," he said. "It's true. Strikes drain the physical, mental, and financial resources of your membership. You are gambling with their security, their futures. If it's possible to avoid all that and still achieve your objective, then do it. It is like going to war. You don't maintain an army, navy, marines, submarines, airplanes, and mountain troops because you dream someday of going into battle and winning with them. You do it in the hope that they will prevent anyone growing strong enough to challenge you; you hope you will never have to use your power. By the same line of reasoning, you take out a life insurance policy to protect your wife until you are 70 years of age. You will be tickled pink if you outlive the policy and never collect."

"Explain the Highway Drivers Council that you formed back in the 1930s," I said.

"Come back into history with me," Beck said. "In 1903 or thereabouts, there was a big Teamsters strike in San Francisco. You'll have to bear in mind that in those days the general trucking industry operated with all horse-drawn equipment. Consequently, there were agreements between the truck operator with horse-drawn equipment and the Teamsters Union. Every bit of freight came off the rails; or came off the waterfront. There was no over-the-road trucking. It took a long time to convince many of our local cartage drivers unions that they should organize over-the-road trucking. As a matter of fact, with the powerful union (Local 85) we had in San Francisco and the one across the bay in Oakland (Local 70), and down through that adjacent industrial area, at first we never organized any over-the-road trucking. We started right here in Seattle; then spread down into Portland. Later we formed the

Highway Drivers Council, with headquarters in San Francisco. The primary objective was not only organizing the over-the-road people, but also the Los Angeles Teamster jurisdiction. Our first big confrontation was in Los Angeles, where we took on the Southern Pacific Railroad, the most powerful company we could find. We knew if we could trounce SPR, we could beat the rest. And we did, too. But, in retrospect, it took a long time for some of our Teamsters to gain strength on the Coast. They had been operating freight via the rails for so long they couldn't get it into their heads that the time had come to fight the railroads if they were to survive. It was an uphill fight for us, but in the end, it was the key to organizing Los Angeles.

"Yes, we fought skull and knuckles sometimes, but we built a powerful organization for wages, hours, and conditions of employment for our union membership. I learned early in life that the administration of a labor union is a business. The average member owns nothing except one thing: his labor. You cut his arms off, and he's an object of charity in the morning."

"The Beck Compound," I said. "The weekly news magazines made much out of it."

"It came about primarily because Mrs. Beck was very sick," Beck explained. "Not many people knew it, but the doctors cautioned me not to change my residence from Seattle to Washington or Indianapolis or any place else in the East. They advised me of this even before I was elected general president. Logically, I wanted to surround our Seattle home with as many relatives and close business associates as possible. So I financed, and helped finance, a number of young fellows who had grown up with my son. There was, for example, Norman Gessert, a cousin of my wife, and his wife and daughter. At that time, he wasn't working full-time with the Teamsters, but he did come in part-time. Then there was Dick Klinge, whom I first met when he was playing football at the University of Washington. I was close to Coach Jimmy Phelan and the Huskies. When Phelan needed money for recruiting ex-

penses, he would drop in on me. I'd get busy on the phone
and by the end of the day I'd have raised $8,000 to $10,000
for the Husky football program. Anyway, Klinge helped
keep me in shape by working out with me. We were early-
morning walking companions. While he was still in college, he worked for the Teamsters only part-time; during
the summers, I got him a job at Sick's Brewery.

"Then there was Al Irvine, also attending Washington.
Al was raised with my son, Dave. I was very fond of him.
After he returned from World War II, I had him named as a
business agent for the Retail Clerks Union, which I organized.

"Joe McEvoy was another resident of Beck's Compound. He was married to my sister's daughter. He, too,
was in college; had served in the military all during the
war. When he married my niece, I secured him employment—not working for the Teamsters, he never did work
for the union—but driving a brewery truck for Sunset
Distributing Company.

"All told, I would say there were no more than three
members of the Compound who were directly associated
with the Teamsters. Actually, the Compound was an investment. Teamster need had nothing to do with it; it was
all family and friends. A lot of folks figured I built the place
as a quarters for the Teamsters, complete with personal
bodyguards and so forth. No, not at all. The only one
qualified to serve as a bodyguard was Klinge. During the
war, he was a fighter pilot and won the Navy's Silver Star
for rescuing personnel under fire.

"The Compound began as raw land. I financed about
five houses out there. The rest of the buildings, where my
wife and young Dave and I lived, I owned myself. Next
door to our house I built a place for my wife's parents.
That's all. I also owned two pieces of lake waterfront, but I
didn't sell them for 10 years. None of this belonged to the
Teamsters. Why, 95 per cent of it was originally purchased
on the installment plan: $10 down and $10 a month. So,
you see, I was even then thinking way ahead."

I asked, "Do you feel that workers are still being exploited in the United States? Are you satisfied with the labor picture?"

"There is some exploitation going on," Beck said. "Where there are no powerful unions to combat them, certain employers try to take advantage of their workers. They have done it for years in the South with black labor; women labor, the same thing. In my opinion, unions should accept women, blacks, and everybody else on identically the same basis; they should be paid the same wages and given the same hours and conditions for the same jobs. However, in certain lines of work I do not agree that women should receive the same wages as men; nor do I believe that men should get the same amount of money in some jobs where women are superior. It must be trial and error; that is the best management and labor can do. Over the next five to 10 years I expect all these injustices to be solved."

"We're coming down to the bottom line, now," I said. "How would you like to be remembered?"

"If I am to be remembered for anything on this earth," he said, "I would like it to be for putting hundreds and hundreds of millions of dollars into the pockets of thousands and thousands of Teamster families so that they could get the maximum enjoyment out of American life; and also for what leadership I gave to the creation of retirement and health and welfare benefits for our members and their families, adding up to *billions*. I think I can take credit for that, and the memory of it will stay with me forever. There were some things I never had time to accomplish, but, on the whole, I think I got around to all the important ones."

"For one man," I said, "you have lived quite a life."

"Yes," he said. "Yes, I have."

"You have been a fighter all your life," I said. "Surely, this must have taught you some important rules to pass along to young people."

"The most important one is never stop trying," he said. "I don't care how great a fighter you are, sooner or later you're going to get floored. The bum will stay down.

The good fighter will get up as soon as he can. The great fighter—the *smart* fighter—will take a nine count and will be back on his feet before the count reaches the fatal 10. That's the way it is in life—*you have to get up at nine.*"

Index